Samuel W. Smith

**Gems From the Tailings**

The Sluice Club

Samuel W. Smith

**Gems From the Tailings**
*The Sluice Club*

ISBN/EAN: 9783743360068

Manufactured in Europe, USA, Canada, Australia, Japa

Cover: Foto ©Thomas Meinert / pixelio.de

Manufactured and distributed by brebook publishing software (www.brebook.com)

Samuel W. Smith

**Gems From the Tailings**

# GEMS FROM THE TAILINGS,

OR

## THE SLUICE CLUB.

BY

SAM W. SMITH,

Author of "Struck Oil," "Tom Bell," "California Girl," etc.

SAN FRANCISCO:
C. W. Gordon, Printer, 326 Sansome Street.
1878.

Entered according to Act of Congress in the year 1875,

BY SAM W. SMITH,

In the office of the Librarian of Congress at Washington.

# GEMS FROM THE TAILINGS.

*Dedicated to*

The old Forty-niners,
And rest of the miners,
No difference what year of arriving.
You're all of a sameness,
Possessing the gameness
That keeps every one of you striving
To find the big nugget,
Though somebody dug it
Out—years ago, you don't mind it.
Saying, "More's in the ground yet
Than's ever been found yet"—
Here's hoping each miner may find it.

# CONTENTS.

|  | PAGE. |
|---|---|
| Preface | 7 |
| Sluice Club—Introduction | 9 |
| The Club | 10 |
| Second Night of the Club | 16 |
| Miners' Cabin | 16 |
| Description of Hon. Judge Baggs | 18 |
| The Judge's Poetic Venture | 20 |
| Characteristics of the Chairman | 25 |
| Red Cap Lake | 27 |
| Peculiarities of N. B. Winkle | 33 |
| Glory all Round | 34 |
| Third Night of the Club—Joseph Briggles | 37 |
| The Last Indian Story | 38 |
| Tom Walker | 43 |
| Lost Cabin | 43 |
| Obituary | 49 |
| The Old Miner | 50 |
| The Hunter's Camp | 53 |
| Doe and Fawn | 57 |
| Death of the Elk | 60 |
| Panther Fight | 63 |
| Old Monte's Bar Fight | 66 |

# CONTENTS.

|  | PAGE. |
|---|---|
| Aztec Maiden | 76 |
| Explanatory Notes | 92 |
| Castle Dome; or, The Gold King | 93 |
| A Centennial Dedication | 104 |
| America | 106 |
| Ossalinta | 121 |
| Explanatory Notes | 129 |
| The Lost One of San Juan | 130 |
| Where is Solitude? | 138 |
| Up and Down Hill | 143 |
| The Times | 145 |
| On Isle of Santa Rosa | 147 |
| Long Years Ago | 149 |
| A Poet's Theme | 151 |
| The Garden of Truth | 154 |
| Songs of the Past | 156 |
| Cherokee Flat | 157 |
| Washed Through the Tunnel | 160 |
| Line of the Ditch | 162 |
| The Granger's Daughter | 164 |
| Living Alone | 166 |
| Brunette Josie | 168 |
| Road of Life | 169 |
| My Picture | 170 |
| Uncle Joe and the Grizzly | 171 |
| Good Dick | 173 |
| Slippery Jim | 176 |
| Happy Jack | 178 |
| Curley Dan | 180 |

# PREFACE.

Fifty years ago a little volume of poems would create a sensation. At the present day it takes fifty sensations to create a small volume; and after the fledgling is born, there are forty-nine and three-quarter chances out of the fifty, that the unknown bird won't live as long as the velocipede excitement. What this will be, who knows? If it is fifty years behind the times, it's too old; if that many years ahead, too new. If exactly between the two, the "Tailings" may have a run equal to some of the old gravel claims on the "blue lead," with the bed-rock pitching. Let it pitch,—will start a tunnel lower down, and make preparations for the next run.

But wait till it is seen how these "gems" will be received. In calling them gems, I do not mean diamonds of the first water, but they are something, as to what, is left to the kind judgment of the public.

S. W. S.

# SLUICE CLUB.

## INTRODUCTION.

Having worked at the occupation of mining for the last twenty years, during that time have prospected, pan'd, rocked, tom'd, sluiced, tunneled, bored, drifted, hydraulic'd, flumed and dam'd (wing-dam), without gaining further distinction than that of a fair prospector, but an unlucky miner; a good stand-by for the trader, but a bad calculator for self; a man who always knew where the gold was, but never found it. Thus, after being passed and raised thro' the various degrees of a miner's life, have, at quite a late hour in the morning, started on the prospect of new diggings; and in locating our claim, selected what we believe is untrodden ground.

So you perceive, this is altogether a new role, our occupation having been that of rolling bowlders. But

> Last winter, there being a wonderful dry,
> The rain didn't come, and no dust for "red eye,"
> While our trader's sign was—"You needn't apply
>   For credit—Come down with the cash."

Now that was the needful that couldn't be found,
For "dust" doesn't raise of itself from the ground,
While all us poor miners were loafing around,
    Waiting for water and wishing a crash

Would fall on that trader, and all of his kind,
Who'd gobbled for years all the "dust" we could find,
And coming hard times, had shut off the wind,
    Leaving no chart for our sailings.

All came to conclusion—"Your liquor's not grub,
Can do without it, if 't comes to the rub,"
And for Winter amusement form'd a SLUICE CLUB,
    'And here's what we saved from the TAILINGS.

## THE CLUB.

Our club being form'd, to get well under way,
We'll first take a glimpse of the players and play,
By giving each name, but their parts and their acts,
We have them wrote down as historical facts.

The first one, of course, was the chairman, Old Doc,
With brain clear as water, clean to the bed rock;
'Twas pleasant to listen to his spicy chat,
Explaining the reasons between "t'.is" and "that;"

How motors might move, if only had motion,
Sailing 'gainst currents and tides of the ocean.
He had a head that was worthy of shoulders
That carried it 'round 'mong gravel and bowlders.

Next on the docket was his honor, Judge Baggs,
Whose long slippery tongue of service ne'er lags,
But ever talking of law's jurisdiction—
Of cases darker and deeper than fiction;
Like Blackstone or Kent, will explain, point by point,
Every limb of the law, dissecting each joint,
Like a Taney or Fields, or his honor, Judge Rhodes,
But broke down at last in explaining the Codes.

The third was Jo Briggles, of talents quite vain,
But all knew poor Joseph had quartz on the brain;
'Twas his thoughts by day and dreams thro' the night,
But all of his ventures went up like a kite,
And now the poor fellow was down in the mouth,
On account of dull times and very great drought;
But there would set, and his eyes fairly glisten,
As much as to say, "I can't talk, but I'll listen."

A list'ner is often preferred to a talker,
As we all found in admitting Tom Walker.
Now Tom, like the rest, was waiting for rain,
And always contending that from the cute pain

In arms or back, that shot round like an arrow,
That we'd have water to work with to-morrow.
'Twas same every night while "Sluice Club" was going.
The rain didn't come, but Tom Walker kept blowing.

Our scholarly mind was Napoleon B. Winkle;
His words were pure coin, no counterfeit tinkle.
Whenever he spoke and whatever he said,
Was certain of hitting the nail on the head.
He'd been a professor of Latin and Greek,
Mythological gods could name for a week,
From Jupiter down, could run the whole gamut,
But used as his clincher, the English god, d—t.

The last one of note was the clerk, or the scribe,
Elected to office without any bribe;
Still was accused of more wisdom than sense,
With ideas of self, both small and immense;
Of traveling and seeing more than he knew;
A fault of too many; how is it with you?
But read and judge, as, of course, you all will,
If he is small potatoes, with few in a hill?

Several besides, who'll appear in a sequel,
If no greater than these, perhaps their equal,
And we hope if they live, will find themselves paid,
For time that they lost and efforts they made.

There may not appear from the "Miners' Sluice Club,"
An original thought, or joke with a nub,
And trader may grumble at losing our dimes,
Already has swore at our jumble of rhymes,

But the last cleaning up, when his claim shall flicker,
He'll find these rhymes are as good as his liquor;
When run thro' the flume, or ground by death's muller,
Swept down or pan'd out, with nary a color,
Will own up at last, not to man, but to devil,
"These fellows had heads exceedingly level;"
And in that hot country, be cured of railings [ings."
'Gainst the "Sluice Club," and "Gems from the Tail-

The chairman then spoke; his words rather got 'em:
"Resolved, every tub stands on its own bottom;
And to each one shall be allotted a night,
To read to the club whate'er he may write;
It must be about something done up in rhyme,
Either ridiculous or on the sublime.
Should any one fail, when the water shall come,
Will have to stand treat to five gallons of rum."

"The game being made, we must all draw for lots."
Use the ten cards of spades; by counting the spots
Every member will know his night to appear;
And boys, I do hope you'll keep your heads clear.

Clerk, take down the numbers; each one knows his place;
The chair has the duce, but the Judge holds the ace.
The club is adjourned, but when we next meet,
The Judge and myself will our pieces repeat."

N. B. Winkle—Mr. Chairman, before we adjourn, I wish to present a series of resolutions.

Tom Walker—I move a resolution be in order.

Judge—A resolution is always in order with miners.

Joe Briggles—I second that motion.

Chairman—Mr. Winkle, it's the decision of the Chair, you present 'em.

Winkle—Mr. President and gentlemen of the "Sluice Club," be it—

*Resolved:*—That on our final "cleaning up," the "tailings" be at the disposal of the Secretary, whom we appoint as our missionary, to go forth and present the gold thereof to all people who are willing to take an interest in the "prospect." To all those who may wish to behold mountain life, whilst reading stories of the wild golden land; listening to men who walk up and down the earth, and from those who delve and dig thro' it; from men who have scattered abroad the golden charm, which has excited the growth of civilized advancement to a height never equaled, once only approached, and that were the days when Cortez and Pizarro poured the wealth of Mexico and riches of the

Incas into the coffers of commerce, and De Soto opened the grandeur of the Mississippi to the eyes of a re-awakened world.

*Resolved:*—There is surrounding our lives, thro' mining lands and woodlands wild, many an unwritten story.

TOM WALKER—Yes sir, I know 'em by the thousands.

WINKLE—Throughout our vast mountain regions are hearts as true, and nerves as tried, as ever trod the quarter-deck or faced the bayonet charge on field of carnage.

JOE BRIGGLES—It takes that sort of men to prospect for quartz.

JUDGE—Or to have heads enough to mine and practice law at the same time.

CHAIR—Gentlemen, order, until the resolutions are read.

WINKLE—*Resolved:*—The language of this club shall be natural, every-day life, just as it is, was, and will be, until generations pass away, and the mountains refuse their wilden charms and hidden wealth. .

JOE BRIGGLES—I move quartz be substituted for the word wealth.

TOM WALKER—I move the whole is adopted.

CHAIRMAN—According to the decision of the chair, they are adopted by parliamentary rule—and the club is adjourned siner diner, till next meeting.

# SECOND NIGHT OF THE CLUB.

## MINERS' CABIN.

Our meetings were held in a cabin of logs,
The mining abode of McFlinn, from the bogs.
Mac was a lover of all kinds of sporting,
Fond of a court room, but fonder of courting;
Would not try rhyming, was out of condition,
But furnish'd room and dudeen ammunition;
Besides a big bottle, if night should be damp,
Now a past luxury in 'most every camp.

His cabin, like others around thro' the mines,
Was clean to a margin, for eyes with thick blinds.
In order to give the reader an idea,
I'll speak of our homes, so cosy and tidy.
As to size and build, it is not much amount,
Only a matter of taste, and taste doesn't count,
Being unornamented, but built for using,
From models so few, it doesn't take choosing.

To form a good chimney is the essential,
And miners who have them are consequential.
Built on the wide guage, and large in their bores,
From huge log and forestick the crackling fire roars,
While long boots and wet clothes, with water soaking,
Give thanks to that fire, as they doze off, smoking;
There our kettle of beans is always in sight,
For bacon and beans are the miner's delight.

The furniture next, are the bunks where we sleep,
And built in all fashions, but most on the cheap,
Just large enough to stretch out in our trouble,
But when a friend comes, of course we must double.
All round thro' the cabin are stools, kegs and boxes,
Some filled with grub, but for chairs, standing proxies,
And setting aside a large board 'gainst the wall,
Which answers for cupboard, a table and all.

There fry-pan and dish-pan are hanging up, brown,
From whence a long stream of dark lard's running down.
Near our can of sour dough and strong saleratus,
Which is foaming already, for slap-jacks await us.
A flick of bacon from string is suspended
By pair of torn pants that long to be mended;
And lying around are lots of old clothes,
Which hard times will make us wear out, we suppose.

And here in a corner, all thrown in a pile,
Are potatoes and flour, our lard can and "ile,"
By a lot of old tools and some worn out hose,
With what else besides the Lord only knows;
Old bottles, old papers, the whole scene completing.
And such was the place our club held its meeting.

## Description of Hon. Judge Baggs.

This being the night for Judge Baggs' appearance, we will simply remark that he is an individual well known all the way from Yreka to Mariposa, from Virginia City to Pioche, and the last letter we received from him was dated at Panamint, where he was to go into business immediately, whether to practice law or mint juleps, failed to state. If the legal fraternity do not recollect having met him at the bars of court rooms, they will readily recognize his description at a thousand bars at least, where his practice is more satisfactory to his own "taste" than lucrative to his acquaintances.

The Judge was born in Georgia, raised in Alabama, went to school with Alexander Stephens, graduated in Arkansas, and migrated to California.

A splendid gentleman, a true sportsman, and one of the best judges of whisky this side of Bowling Green, Kentucky. If his sublimity is not of the highest order, his rudeness is never of the lowest grade. One of your good, old fashioned, how come you so, sort of fellows that you best borrow from, than lend money to. That night

> The Judge had come in, dressed neat as a pin,
> In trowsers of duck, with handkerchief stuck
>     In side pocket of gray mining shirt.
> His face, a broad grin, from cheek to chin,
> With fine ruddy nose, as pink as the rose,
>     Causing blood to show plainer than dirt.

The Chairman spoke: "The meeting's in order.
Please read the minutes, Mr. Recorder."
That being thro' with, the Judge took his stand
On top of a box, imposingly grand.
He first gave a hem, and then gave a haw,
Raising right hand as tho' pleading the law;
Went sailing in boldly, with ease and grace,
As tho' he were in for a two-forty race.

## The Judge's Poetic Venture.

I went to the city one summer,
    'Twas that time I started for fame.
And I didn't stay long, till a bummer
    Gave me right to share with his name.

Thus it was, I soon gained a standing,
    Free lunch tables could stand beside,
I own, it warn't very commanding,
    But whar ar' the bummer what's died?

I only took such as was offered,
    Free lunches as well as free shows;
Can't never refuse what ar' proffered;
    With a judge, why, everything goes.

One night I drop'd in at a lecture,
    To hear about anything new;
'Twas thar that I heard a conjecture,
    Which'd make any rhymster feel blue.

He war telling: "This grand, golden land,
    Was fairest and brightest of earth,
And for ages and all time 'twould stand,
    As a home for poetical birth.

"But a miner, could not be a poet;
　　Their thoughts ar' too low and grov'ling,
For truth of the point, he could show it,
　　In dirt they ar' always shov'ling.

"And whenever find a bright valley,
　　Whar' nature sings sweet in her lay,
Thar's no standing round on the dally,
　　But dig it and wash it away.

"What a poet would worship, and paint
　　In fanciful thoughts of the mind,
The cold miner doth leave but a taint
　　Of bed-rock and pit-holes behind."

I'd carried with me from the mountains,
　　A bundle of papers and trash,
Which told about clear, sparkling fountains,
　　That flowed over rocks with a dash;

And into great rivers went flowing,
　　On, on, to the ocean of time,
Thro' valleys where nature war glowing
　　Far brighter than Italy's clime.

They told of green, flowering hillsides,
　　All dotted with silk, mossy trees;
Of pure, yellow gold of the rill-sides,
　　That roll'd up the trade of the seas,

With her ten thousands ships for a fleet,
    Thar banners of plenty unfurl'd,
Whar Orient and Occident meet,
    With a grand' "How d'y do?" to the world.

But after that lecture war well through,
    I went to my cold, little room,
Where all my bright hopes just fell thro';
    I had gone to my ink-slinging tomb.

Thar looked over my bundle of stuff,
    Selected what orter be good,
Next day took it to General Puff,
    Who head of the publishers stood;

Only a glance, and did that for show,
    Then tossing it back with a scorn;
"My dear fellow, 'tis entirely too low
    For columns of *The Golden Horn*."

By the lecturer and critic both,
    I felt considerably jilted,
Making tracks for my room, with an oath,
    But thar's the place that I wilted.

My landlady asked for the rent,
    Close dealer was M'lle DeToots,
And as I couldn't raise nary red cent,
    She raised me clear out of my boots.

Had to leave my dear calf-skins in soak,
    Putting on my old, worn-out shoes,
War o' leaving the city dead broke,
    And may be, I hadn't the blues.

But I chanced to meet one Mr. Hart,
    Don't know, but think he played cards,
As a writer, he war making a start,
    And I called him one o' my pards.

We dickered, I sold him my trash,
    To most any terms would agree ;
I asked him: " Whar'd you get all that cash?"
    He whispered, a " Heathen Chinee."

I got back to the mines by a scratch,
    With feelings all gone of sublime,
And here I shall stay, still keeping batch,
    Till pan'd out by old Father Time.

    But my friend, Mr Hart,
    After making his start,
Became a great poet contractor ;
    Was to furnish the brain
    For an Atlantic train,
That's run by a huge Boston factor.

On his getting down east,
His talent thar ceased,
But he played out his hand on a bluff,
Soon found in that climate,
His muse wouldn't rhyme it,
So, onrolling my bundle of stuff,

He run that thro' the mill,
The huge contract to fill,
But the critics went after him lots,
And 'twas thus in the end,
That my talented friend
Went to reading about Argonauts.

So the members will please ease me down,
As poetry is not my forte;
If the Club lasts, may do something brown,
Before the next setting of Court.

---

Joe Briggles arose: "Mr. Chairman, I move,
In order to show our respects and approve,
I be 'lowed to present the Judge my mortar,
In which I pound quartz."
Tom Walker replied: "I think we orter
Present two quarts, to be drank without water,
To keep him in sorts."

The Chairman then spoke: "The Judge has done well,
But with his talents, might have done better.
I was really hopeful that he would tell
The pretty story of the love letter
Which he received from M'lle DeToots,
When she sent photographs of his lost boots;
But time hurries on, 'tis getting toward 'nine.'
The club can listen to this ' thing ' of mine."

## Characteristics of the Chairman.

Before hearing the Chairman's production, it might be proper to state some of his peculiar peculiarities. He is a great stickler for "Chinee cheap labor," because his brother-in-law owns the trading post, and makes two cents clean profit on loud smelling fish and Cheap John rice. He is also a great admirer of the red man, and thinks Miss Red Man has a heart as large as an apple dumpling, and tender as a seed cucumber. Generally in good humor about three days out of the year, and during the other three hundred and sixty-two, can out snarl and out growl a patent bull dog, with shaved head and sore ears.

Reads the newspapers for no other purpose than to find out how many preachers have fallen from grace, what lawyers have sworn to false statements, which insurance company has failed, and constantly expecting to find that Congress has sold the Patent Office for a railroad depot.

In his general estimation, everybody is dishonest, and the whole world is on the highway to the sulphurous abodes of hereafter. In fact, if Old Doc had his way, would hang every dishonest man in the nation, and, suppose he could, there wouldn't be timber enough left to form a working Board of Supervisors, or our next Legislature.

No, no, Mr. Chairman, your doctrine will never do. The world is about as honest as it ever was. Jacob's "ring" streaked and striped speculation on Father Laban was about as large, reckoning the time it happened, as the "ring" streaked and speckled speculators made out of the "Big Bonanza." No great difference in the stories, except that one happened a long time ago, and the other quite recently.

But notwithstanding all of Old Doc's eccentricities, he presented a very readable verse, which is entitled

## RED CAP LAKE.

At eve, two hunters, tired and sore,
Were making camp near lakelet shore ;
'Twas 'neath the Klamath mountain crest,
Where they were seeking night of rest.
A forest of fair Silvia's order,
Made for lake a pretty border,
Shutting in its glistening spray,
For fear a drop might steal away.

The east stood ope'd to gladden'd sight,
Full high above, with rocky height,
As tho' to guard that lovely lake,
So nearly hid, mid fern and brake.
But when the sun rose high and bold,
That silvery sheet did crag enfold,
To mirror back each shadowy peak,
In signs of love it could not speak.

A wild lone spot, in truth I tell
The hunters' camp, 'tis known full well ;
A place that much the red men fear,

In mournful story you shall hear,—
A Hoopa brave was hunting nigh,
Their camp-fire smoke did quickly spy,
He came and spoke, all in a breath,
" Move quick, or night will bring sure death."

Each hunter sprang and grasp'd his arms,
What danger's near, whence cometh harm?
We've here but two, but here we'll stay
Till might 'gainst right shall drive us 'way."

" There is no danger you can ween,
'Tis from power that is unseen,
That creepeth long, like nightly dew,
'Twould fall on me, 'twill fall on you,
It raiseth from pale Red Cap Lake,
And cometh up the mountain break."

" There, see it, 'tis coming,
　　It moves like a cloud,
Each forest tree's bending,
　　Each bough with it bow'd.
Come quickly, come quickly,
　　'Twill camp-fire enshroud,—
'Tis breath of Ca-tonk-wa,
　　Bode of all evil,
It's moving, yes coming,
　　Heap, Indian devil."

Then Hoopa brave all quickly fled,
With fleetest foot, ne'er turn'd his head,
While our two hunters soon did make
A meal, from juicy venison steak.

Their pipes were filled, then a smoke,
Tales of the day and hunter's joke;
While each one spoke in idle jeer,
Of Indian and his foolish fear;—
Mankind's many superstitions,
  Outside, too, of wild conditions,—
And thus they talk'd of ghostly fright,
'Till dusk chang'd with coming night.

With moss and leaves, a bed was made,
Beneath the fir-tree's nightly shade;
There musing o'er a hunter's spoil,
They rested from their daily toil,
And watching starlight's twinkling gleams,
Soon floated off to land of dreams.
As the night wan'd, the moon arose,
With light soft mellow'd from the snows
Of Klamath's glinted mountain peak,
Each hunter woke, but not to speak.

They saw a bright form,
   Growing brighter and brighter,
As the moon's silver light
   Made it lighter and lighter;
A something was there,
   Not an ideal human,
Yet in appearing
   Very image of woman;
And stretching forth arms,
   Said, "I am coming to take,
One of you hunters
   To my crystal homed lake."

"Years have I lived,
   Round Klamath and Trinity,
Long have been seeking
   To find my affinity,
And now being found
   In his love I must revel,
No longer embracing
   The cold Indian devil,—
One shall go with me
   To bright waters below,
I'll no longer live
   Lonely in lakelet of snow."

One hunter arose,
  Said, "My dear, I declare,
If you are a nymph,
  You're both fragile and fair;
But be what you will,
  Sprite, goblin or maid,
Mine eyes ne'er beheld
  Anything I'm afraid,
Please let me approach
  To know your construction,
I'll take it quite kind,
  Well, an introduction."

He spoke nothing more ;
  Transfixed in affright,.
Was caught in the arms
  Of the water nymph sprite,
Quickly both vanish'd
  In the darkness of night.

Of his dear comrade, all bereft,
One hunter 'lone, was lonely left,
Who hid himself in rocky cleft,
With full intent, to save his bacon ;

His hours were spent in thoughtful waking,
At the sad bent that things were taking.
He saw his friend in shadowy keeping,
With watery eyes, all wildly weeping
On lakelet bed, so coldly sleeping.

The longest night must wear away,
And he felt bold, as sunlit ray
Dispell'd all spirit, light and airy ;
Our hero did not longer tarry,
But quickly forth was on a tramp,
He hurried to the Red man's camp,—
And there what did his glad eyes see,
His friend quite safe in the ranch'rie.

And sprite of the night
  Which his wild eyes saw,
By the morning light,
  Was a strip'd face squaw.

As this was the Chairman's poetic production,
None criticised or drew a deduction
But Walker, who was as sour as sour sorrel,
Was sour enough, to put in this sour moral.

"In darkness of night, eyes often deceive us,
And friends whom we trust ofttimes will leave us;
If by Darwin's rule, we were plac'd on the scales,
Some men are as low as the beasts that wear ears."

Nothing further—the Chairman arose,
Blush on his face, that reach'd to the nose;
"The Club is done, for a time, with small-fry,
We'll hear from Winkle—his subject is high."

## N. B. WINKLE.

Our man Winkle, as heretofore stated, is a scholar, and as a natural consequence, is a gentleman. This rule is said to hold good in all cases, except that of Doctor Johnson and Joshua Billings. The first was a fine scholar, but a coarse gentleman, and the last is a splendid gentleman, but has the name of being a very dull scholar, especially in orthography.

Winkle is a great reader; has read about everything, from the sparkling pages of the highest old authors, down even to the editorial notes in the *Alta California*. He can tell the day of the month that Columbus broke the egg, and day of the week the last acrobat broke his neck. Besides, can come as near demonstrating the properties of distilled lightning as any philosopher that ever attempted to explain its exhilarating tendencies.

His imagination borders slightly on the sublime, and the following production should entitle him to a life membership in the Society of High Jinks:

## GLORY ALL ROUND.

One crystal air'd evening, on summit divide,
　The sun gently moving away to its rest,
Like a round globe of gold, lay on ocean's tide,
Not offering to sink, but seeming to glide,
　Still farther and farther away in the west,
　While Nature in garb of her night clothes had dress'd,
And buttoned them on, with diamond lit stars,—
　With Orion's belt, had she girded her waist,
And placed on her bosom the breast-plate of Mars;
　Lovely Venus appeared so modestly chaste,
That Jupiter most benignly looked down,
And Saturn presented his rings for a crown.

O'er the plains, in the east, now slowly arose
　A circle of silver, with pale glinted light,
Appeared but a moment, then plainer it shows,
That a round orb it will quickly disclose.

There it was, the full moon, the queen of the night,
"Glory all round," thus I cried, what a sight!
What eye hath beheld it before on this earth?
Here to raptured gaze, are stars, moon and sun,
They once sang together at creation's birth.
And now again chanting their anthems as one,—
It was but a moment, the sun pass'd away,
Scarce leaving a glimmer to show her last ray.


You may talk, if you will, of Italy's skies,
Of sunny valed France, with air soft and bland,
Of Spain's azure clouds, with purple hued dyes,
Of Norway's glory, aurorial sunrise,
But here in our own unpraised golden land,
Is air that is brighter, a scenery more grand,
Than the poets of past, e'en thought in their lay,
Could ever be seen by mortality's eyes,
Where the Queen of the night, and King of the day
Are singing their songs with the stars of the skies;
Thus bidding the world, come forth and behold
My crystal air'd skies, ere you worship my gold.


Come forth and behold the last land of the west,
Where nature hath planted her roses of wealth,
And lingering to trail, fanned and caress'd
Her latest loved work, till the air she'd bless'd,

With nightly land breezes, from mountains by stealth,
To meet kiss of ocean's invigoring health,
And to finish it all, she lavish'd around,
  Her forests of trees and treasures of flowers,
What ever was planted in life giving ground,
  Sprang into bloom by Omnipotent powers,
And husbandman learns that aside from her gold,
There is sure return for a fair hundred fold.

You may call her works grand, or call them sublime,
  Each word-painted picture most surely falls low,
But when she is worshipped in on-coming time,
In true adoration as earth's fairest clime,
  Then canvass shall sparkle, her beauties to show,
  But ne'er can delineate nature's pure glow
That is beheld from each grand mountain chain,
  Whence eye drinketh in such visions of sight,
O'er fields of the vine and treasured land grain,
  The soul cries Eureka, enraptur'd delight,
Here finished creation hath lavishly crown'd,
Her fairest and brightest, with "Glory all round."

---

The Chairman arose, with magnanimity;
"Here is indeed the height of sublimity,
Cloud-colored, sun-dyed, no extravaganza,
But the afflatus of poetic fancy;

Such as must stand 'gainst the critics out-pouring,
Altogether too grand for common place soaring,
Before hearing others the Club will adjourn,
Remember next meeting is Briggles' turn.

## THIRD NIGHT OF THE CLUB.

### JOE BRIGGLES.

The Club met with expectations of hearing something grandiloquent from Mr. Briggles. He had been steadily writing, re-writing and taking notes, for the last three weeks, and repeatedly told Old Doc that he had the most remarkable poem, founded on fact, that had been written since the discovery of Quartz.

Joe, as you are aware, had a little soft spot in his head, where many others have a very large one. 'Twas the organ of quartz. Most of our modern phrenologists have failed to place it properly on their charts. But almost any Californian knows its exact location: it is situated below common sense, just between wild-cat and expectation.

It has been very beneficial to Jones, but lightning on Briggles. It has made its hundred millionaires, but will leave a million pauper-heirs, who in time will regrasp the wealth that is building up the lords to-day.

So if our friend's story is soft, it must be set against the universal growing organ of quartziveitiveness.

## THE LAST INDIAN STORY.

In prospecting for quartz
   O'er the New River hills,
That country of grandeur,
   Wild streamlets, bold rills,
Where nature is nature,
   As there you will find her,
And scorning the shackles
   With which man would bind her.

'Twas there I came across
   Indian Mau-we-mar,
The last one of his tribe,
   A seery old dreamer,
"One eye" being sightless,
   Head wrinkled and hoary,
And here's what he told me,
   The last Indian story.

"Many moons have pass'd, and winters of snow,
    And my tribe have all melted away,
A few more short moons Mau-we-mar must go,
    He lingers here only a day.

"But when he was young, his people were great,
    With their camp-fires on hill-sides and stream,
The pale faces came and woe was their fate,
    Soon were fading away like a dream.

"But in that sad dream, mine eyes yet behold,
    Fair Na-o-ma, the bride of my choice,
Her eyes like the fawn, her face purest gold,
    And a sweet singing bird, was her voice.

" Her father was Chief of New River band,
    An' proud of his beautiful daughter,
He knew she was fairest in all the land,
    Full many a young brave had sought her.

" She dwelt by yon cliff, near tall sugar pine,
    You see towering there like a reed ;
That I might win her and say she was mine,
    I would have to do some daring deed.

"That time a monster, the great Kickaboo,
    On many young children did feast,
And our brightest boys, and fairest maids too,
    Were devour'd by that horrible beast.

"A council was held, the Chief there did say,
  "Na-o-ma, my daughter, I'll give her,
To any young brave, who'll follow and slay
  The ravenous beast of New River."

"I had prepar'd one hundred great arrows,
  Made true by the artist Mal-da-am,
Determined to end our nation's sorrows,
  Would track home the beast, and then slay him.

"You've seen my long bow, it now is unstrung,
  Yes, you know its great size and length,
Mau-we-mar is old, but when he was young,
  Ah, to double it back, had the strength.

"Bidding Na-o-ma and kindred adieu,
  Armed with my bow and full quiver,
I started in search of Old Kickaboo,
  Away towards head of the river.

"Found where he lived, in cañon rocky,
  Rough, rugged, there, no spot is level,
The Indians call it Bo-ham-a-chock-y,
  The white man has named it devil.*

---

\* Devil's Cañon.

"When sighting the monster, my blood ran cold,
   Yes, as cold as the ice freezing snow,
One thought, 'twas Na-o-ma, each arrow told,
   As a line streamed out from my bow.

" On came the beast, with his terrible cry,
   For Mau-we-mar, there was no retreat,
His great cragged horn tore out this eye,
   As the monster fell dead at my feet.

" Yes, there lay the beast, with bloody mouth wide,
   Every arrow had gone to its place,
With horrible groans, great Kickaboo died,
   'Twas the last of the Kickaboo race.

" He'd horns like an elk, and head as a bear,
   With four flaming eyes in his head,
And two rows of teeth, one sharp and one square,
   What a sight 'twas to see him when dead.

" He could walk upon fours, or walk on two,
   And flew like a bird when he ran,
That's why we called him the Old Kickaboo,
   For he was both a beast and a man.

" My victory over, oh what a feast,
   Eating and dancing a whole moon thro',
Until devouring the whole of the beast,
   Yes, we ate up the last Kickaboo."

The Indian was done, then drawing a sigh,
   And here are the last words he spoke,
"Mau-we-mar heap hungry, eat 'em bime bye,
   You give him tobacker, he smoke."

---

The Chairman spoke up, with sarcastic grin ;
"Why, my dear Briggles, your story's too thin ;
When writing 'bout Indians, spread it on thick,
Of the tame savage, the public are sick,
But noble Red men, to th' wild manner born,
That's a theme for a poet—

          "Yes, in a horn,"
Spoke up Tom Walker, "I think that the Chair ;
Had best run with Diggers, put tar on his hair.
Glorified Indian is all very fine,
The Chair can have his'n, I want none in mine ;
Their constant praises may go to the dogs,
Better eat bacon and poetise hogs.

Old Doc replied, "That's insolent punning,
You're only clogging the 'sluice,' while running.
The rule of the Club, 'twas left for the Chair
To criticise openly, freely and fair ;
As you forever wish to be gabbing
Just take your turn and read the "Lost Cabin."

## TOM WALKER.

Tom Walker, who has frequently been noticed, was descended from the old thorough-bred down East stock, born in the country and raised in the woods. Christianed after Irving's Tom Walker, whom you recollect went to the devil, after living luxuriously for a short time on treasure trove, of famous Captain Kidd.

Our Tom has not as yet followed in the footsteps of his namesake, but if he thought there were new diggings in that country, he'd shoulder his blankets and start to-morrow. If the climate should happen to be warm enough to do without them, he'd trade them for an extension on the first claim located.

Tom is one of our regular, representative miners, a little rough, but as ready to pungle with his means, from a true heart, as is a good claim. Loves fair-dealing, honest morality, and pure friendship; but hates Indians, Chinamen, small-pox and fleas. He has hunted longer and more of it, for the "lost cabin," than any two men in California, and will swear or fight anytime for truth of his story—which is

## THE LOST CABIN.

Did you ever hear tell 'bout the Lost Diggings?
But no difference; the story I'll tell,
'Twas the Summer I was partner of Wiggins,
When we prospected round a long spell.

We went up Squaw Creek and river McCloud,
    They are both tributaries of Pit,
We had the true bearing as we allowed,
    And you bet, you, the git up and git.

'Twas on that same trip, we came across Miller,
    Who now is the Sierra poet;
No use o' talking, sometimes the Fool-killer
    Lets people grow up, and out grow it.

That chap was living, like the rest of his band,
    On acorns and roasted buckeyes,
You might call his wigwam, both gaudy and grand,
    But need look thro' some poetic guise.

Manzanitas they reckon'd bully cha-muck,
    All too lazy to hunt for much game,
Were laying 'round camp and waiting for luck,
    'Till the season of grasshoppers came.

It was there he learned so much about "Lo,"
    Gaining poetic knowledge beside,
By winning the love of the beauty "So-ho,"
    His heroined Kit Carson bride.

Her tresses were dark, like a black horses' mane,
    With pretty red eyes quite inflamed,
Oh, she would the soul of a poet enchain,
    At least she did one we have named.

But there's no judging taste ; who could then know,
    That the man was really thinking
Of things very high, while from fountain so low,
    His muse with his sow-how* was drinking.

He did, that's enough, may the gods place his name
    Along side of some sort of figure,
But if it's inscribed on the Temple of Fame,
    How far should it be from a Digger ?

But here's a digression, I'll back if I can,
    Yet 'twould have been very ungallant,
Not to have spoken of a wonderful man,
    Whom I've seen and know has some talent.

It wasn't that Summer, but the Summer before,
    That the news was all bruited around,
About lucky miners—"a good thing once more ;"
    Yes, the tallest of diggings had found.

They came from the mountains, pretending affright,
    Said Injuns were after 'em surely ;
Had buried their dust away in the night,
    If they did, its for all time securely.

---

\* A splendid dish—generally soup compounded of dried acorns and grasshoppers.

They were going back again in the Spring,
   To continue work on their diggins,
Two miners determined to find out the thing,
   You know it was me an' Old Wiggins.

Old Wiggins carried the highest old rifle;
   Why, they used to have guns in those days;
Not your rattle-trap, or thing-magig trifle,
   That are made now to shoot both ways.

She'd mark of St. Louis, made by Old Hawkin,
   And carried a clean ounce of lead;
Whenever she spoke, well, no use o' talkin,'
   'Twas a sure thing, that something was dead.

Oh, but wasn't he proud, when he'd shoulder Beauty;
   Kept her all tidy and scrubbed out,
Ready and loaded at all times for duty,
   And many a red skin she rubbed out.

We followed their track, as following a deer,
   O'er mountain, thro' valley and jungle,
No difference to us, how far or how near,
   Would look for the thing till 'twould pungle.

We found where they camp'd, in a low hidden swale,
   Watched them for weeks, only reason,
Were going to find out the truth of their tale,
   If it took the whole of the season.

Once I wished to go back, but Wiggins said,
"I think they are snakes that need watching,
We'll stay till we see if a little cold lead
Won't fit 'em as well as a scotching."

They had been disguised for the last few days,
Painted and dressed like the Modoc scamp,
As we could plain see by the sun's shining rays,
As we lay in our own hidden camp.

Their abode was close to the Oregon trail;
Bang, bang, bang, went three rifles one morning,
Old Wiggins jumped, "Thar ar blood on the gale,
Last night I dreamed o' this warning."

It was sure enough—from the place where we stood,
Could see the true wealth of their diggings,
They were panning out men, their claim was the road,
It had long been opinion of Wiggins.

He told me, "come on, we'll dry up that sluice,
Oh, what a bust, of a rich mining camp, [loose,
We'll make them three ruffians think h—l has broke
And the Devil is out on a tramp."

Quick to our places, and taking our stands
Where their trail came towards us, near straight;
The three ruffians came 'long with blood on their hands,
Cursed wolves, deserving their fate.

My partner was ready and Beauty quick spoke,
  In a voice that was slightly stunning;
You'd ought to been there, seen the lift of her smoke,
  And the little red sluice heads running.

Just like three dead Injuns, in dresses uncouth,
  Of their crimes there are no accountin',
'Twas an eye for an eye, a tooth for a tooth,
  You know that's the law of the mountain.

There, you have the "lost cabin," from glitter and gilt,
  And those robbers found out to their cost,
No diggings were there, and no cabin was built,
  Therefore I don't think it was lost.

## CHAIRMAN.

" 'Tis the Chairman's opinion that your effusion,
Would have been better had made no allusion
    'Gainst the author of Sierra songs;
We're all aware that no one can live
So perfect, as not at some time to give
    A chance to be accused of wrongs.

## TOM.

I made no accusings, spoke only the truth,
Of what I beheld of the man in his youth,
  If 'twere rights, or 'twere wrongs,
    The whole world may know it,
  While they're praising the songs
    Of the Sierra poet;
And the Chairman needn't raise such a clatter,
He's had some in his'n, that's what's the matter."


OBITUARY.—Old Doc said he'd stand no further insults; declared the Club dissolved, tore up the Constitution, and left in high dudgeon.

What mighty events transpire from little causes; none had foreseen it, none were prepared for the final dissolution. But so it was, the President was gone, the Constitution destroyed and the Sluice Club only a thing of the past. Ex-members were dumb-founded; spectators shocked. Each still had their hats and heads full of literary matter, and according to previous resotions, all, all must be thrown into the common heap of "tailings" of the "Sluice Club," to become the sole property of the Secretary.

Oh, what a pile; oh what a mass of grit, of dirt, of sand, of broken bed-rock, drift, and rotten bowlders.

It appeared as tho' the whole community had run wild on jungling rhyme, or roaring verse. The subjects were generally without beginning or ending, head or tail. But that is not to be wondered at when you consider they are—simply Tailings from the Sluice Club.

The work of the Secretary was of no light order; must "pan out" and sort over the same, retaining the "prospects" and "Gems."

The first picking therefrom, was without title, name or authorship—probably written by some good old miner whose best days are numbered with the past, and we have Christianed it

## THE OLD MINER.

I am sure I should pass for a miner,
    For I've min'd for years twenty-two,
Though not quite an Old Forty-nine'er,
    For learning the trade that should do.

When I first came into the gold lan',
    Luck sat by my side every week,
And Saturday night, why my old pan,
    Looked as tho' it had struck a good streak.

I had money to keep and to spend,
    And money to buy and to pay,
I had money to sink and to lend,
    But nary to gamble away.

I was hoarding my wealth for old age,
    Yes, hoarding it 'gainst all the fates,
For the purpose to build a gold cage,
    For birdie I'd left in the States.

I had found a rich placer of gold,
    In a range where miners did say,
"'To work there, you'll get badly sold,
    For broken black bed-rock don't pay."

It was feruenst of what now is Gold Hill,
    That time 'twas a wild looking spot,
By the place there's a pounding quartz mill,
    And I don't know what else they haint got.

There I built me a cabin of brush,
    And laid in my grub for a while,
I was happy and sang like a thrush,
    So fast was I making my pile.

I brought my huge sack full to town,
    And left it with Adams & Co.,
On the very next coach to go down,
    But somehow it happened just so—

I received a letter by mail,
    It came along infernal slow,
But it told me, my own Lizzy Gale,
    Was mated just nine months ago.

I felt bad from my head to my toes,
    Felt bad from my stomach to heel,
Felt so bad, that the Lord only knows,
    How bad a poor fellow can feel.

I wished that the whole world would sink,
    And everything turn upside down,
Then to drown it, I took a big drink,
    And soon went a snorting 'bout town.

Quitting work—'twas an infernal shame—
    Went round with a down hanging lip,
Some miners had jumped my old claim,
    And that's how I lost my old nip.

My boat floated on without oars,
    With life I was fairly disgusted
Somehow, it never rains, but it pours,
    Then Adams & Co., they went busted.

Since then its from worse to no better,
    Never had a claim worth a " gol darn."
All come from the Lizzy Gale letter,
    I hope she may yet read this yarn.

# THE HUNTER'S CAMP.

In the Mendocino mountains,
    Before the ranchmen found us,
There we dwelt as happy hunters,
    With plenty all around us.

We had fallen there together
    Like severed leaves from trees,
Some from o'er the sandy deserts,
    Some from homes beyond the seas.

But no difference whence our coming,
    Each was there, as nature's child,
And affections twin'd together,
    Thro' the mountain's wooded wild.

'Tis away from population,
    Afar from moneyed mart,
Where our feelings swell most kindly,
    Welling forth from heart to heart.

True, each had their little foibles,
    Gave and taking jokes for fun,
But as ready to forgive them,
    As were ready with their gun.

We had Jack, the jolly sailor,
    Who had left the salty seas,
To salt down our deer and elk meat,
    For our winter bread and cheese.

Curly headed little Johnny,
    A bright graduate from Yale,
Who was barely a five-footer,
    But from bear would never quail.

And to keep our morals perfect,
    Had good old Parson Sides,
Who once had worked at saving souls,
    He works now at saving hides.

Next was civil Zacharias,
    Had been civil engineer,
But left, civil home and country,
    Just to civilize us here.

With the rest, a playful sportsman,
    Who had been Old Monte's slave,
But now must bar his door 'gainst "bar,"
    His barred in pot to save.

Among the last, a broken miner,
    Who had run things in the ground;
He run the bullets, run the camp,
    While the rest were running 'round.

There our time sped bright and happy,
   And till yet how oft I yearn,
To live those loved days over,
   But alas! they'll ne'er return.

'Tis among those dear companions,
   Past time hath wrought its changes,
And like elk, the early hunters,
   Have left the mountain ranges.

Some have gone to distant countries,
   Some other wilds have found,
And some I trust are living now
   In the happy hunting ground.

But till yet, how oft I'm thinking,
   Of those night times whiled away,
With the many hunting stories
   And adventures of the day.

One eve, I still remember,
In purple brown September;
All sparkling, cheerful humor,
No complaints, pains or tumor,
Were spoken of as ailings;
And Jack for once left sailings,
For some other time and place,
And that night took up the chase.

Those men uncouthly 'pearing,
Oft language used worth hearing;
If it were but rightly sifted,
No doubt would pass as highly gifted.

But I'll state in this connection,
   That it's all from recollection,
And if there's found both beams and motes,
   Old Memory says, "I've lost my notes."

'Tis from memories archives,
   We'll cull what'er we can,
Not their written storied lives,
   But 'venture of each man.

Should they be worth hearing,
   Perhaps some other time,
May have a reappearing
   On future page of rhyme.

---

Of those adventures we'll begin,
Let each and each, their stories spin;
There sat the hunters 'round the fire,
As it burned low, would move nigher,
To punch a brand or light a pipe;
In talking humor all were ripe;
The stories told are hard to beat.
At least, to me, they were a treat.

'Twas college boy that made the start,
He'd frame of steel, but then his heart
Was gentle, loving, warm and kind,
And gained its impulse from his mind.
That mind was formed from balanced brain,
So pure in thought, that wrong gave pain ;
From what was right, would never swerve,
To stand by it, he had the nerve.

## THE DOE AND FAWN.

" This morn in hunting o'er a lawn,
I saw a pretty spotted fawn,
That frisk'd around with doe so sleek,
Which seemed to watch and almost speak.
I thought while hidden in that wildwood,
Of mother mine and early childhood,
How she had watched my every move,
With her maternal fondling love.

" There stood the doe, to guard her child,
Appearing gentle, yet all wild;

When e'er from pine tree drop'd a burr,
Or any leaflet chanced to stir,
Or if a birdling changed its song,
Her fine arched neck, so lithe and strong,
Would 'sume that pretty poising curve,
And the quick tension of each nerve
You see in timid, watchful deer,
A spring for life, when danger's near.

"In watching her it paid me well,
If only could her thinking tell,
'Twould pay you, too, to hear it told,
But still 'twould be the story old;
That story came from power above,
A standing truth of mother's love.
That's ever same without a change,
In city's hum, or mountain range.

"I looked at fawn, then at the mother,
Their loving lives were in each other;
For sport or hunger ne'er have I
Caused innocents like those to die.
I'll slay a buck, where'er I find it,
His bleating death cry, never mind it;
But gentle mother, pretty fawn,
I left them both upon the lawn.

" But returning back towards camp,
I was well paid for my long tramp,
In having chance and having luck,
To kill a noble six-point buck.
I shot him on the upward bound;
'Twas his last leap, turned clear 'round,
His head behind, his feet towards sky,
Yes there my gallant prize did lie.

"I'm truly proud of that bold shot,
His neck was broken on the spot;
In weight I know, he's hard to beat,
Will go two-fifty, clean and neat.
With antler'd horns, velvet glossy,
Like little oaks, silken mossy,
His hair so sleek, all downy blue,
Such deer as he are very few.

" I left him safe from roaming bear,
Placing two sticks across him square ;
For bear and devil are the same,
They fear a cross, are not to blame,
But I must own, in Christian shame,
'Tis a low trick, but saves high game ;
My story's thro', I see Jack's itching
To tell a yarn, his mouth is twitching."

## DEATH OF THE ELK.

Jack said, " I must say your yarn's rather tame;
　　But we shouldn't expect very much
From you pot-hunters, who hunt little game,
　　I never waste powder on such.
You put me in mind of a school-boy's zest,
　　With his little gun out "bobbin,"
Is almost too good to rob a bird's nest,
　　But shoots off head of "cock robin."

"This morning, hunting up blue-brush divide,
　　A band of fine fellows I struck,
There was not an elk, around that hillside
　　But'd weigh at least three times your buck.
There were forty-one, I counted them pass,
　　Being all in range of a shot,
I laying low, in a forest of grass,
　　To pick out my choice of the lot.

"Some of you hunters who style yourselves men,
　　Would have began killing for fun,
Making green hillside an elk slaughter pen,
　　To brag about what you had done.

Robbing our mountains of this kind of game,
  And leaving the woodlands all lone,
I say to you all, 'tis a sin and shame—
  That any true sportsman will own.

" As fine herd as that you'll not often see,
  All bulls, with their great toppling horns,
Each stepping around, so proudly and free,
  As tramping the ground that he scorns.
Scorning the earth, where they're placing their feet,
  With bold toss of head as to say,
'I'm brave, but courage belongs to the fleet-
  Footed, over hills far away.' "

" While musing thus, they were feeding quite near,
  My grass-spot slightly encroaching;
I wished; oh, could old Billy Shakespeare,
  Have seen such a sight while poaching.
We'd have 'Elk plays,' surpassing Othello,
  Casting in shade Richard the Third,
Each of these elk on the stage could bellow,
  What glorious chance for the 'herd.'

" But star of the band, must play his last part,
  My finger impatiently burned,
As gave a shot that crashed thro' his heart,
  But he stood as if unconcerned.

Ne'er flinching muscle, or batting an eye,
    Grandly as an ideal lion,
Seeming to say, "'tis the bite of a fly,"
    Yet he was standing up dying.

" While his very life blood was oozing fast,
    With grandeur his neck was raised high,
Appearance and actions spoke to the last,
    ' I'll hold up my head till I die.'
On haunches he soon began to give way,
    Each moment lower and lower,
There in his death, did as gracefully lay,
    As though he were living once more.

" He is fully as large as there's any need,
    Fat as bullock fed in a stall,
Will pull down nine hundred, he will indeed,
    For elk that is not very small.
I left the old dog, poor fellow's quite lame,
    But will stay until I get back,
To-morrow we'll go for that noble game,
    'Twill take all the mules in the pack.

## A PANTHER FIGHT.

Parson Sides, our buck-skin tanner,
Next spoke up, in olden manner;
With hard-shell phrase and drawling tone,
As though his thorax was a bone,
An' he was blowing marrow through it,
Just because he had to do it.
His tales, mostly on romantic,
At times, bordering on gigantic;
Like Washington, with honor high,
Old Sides could never tell a lie.


" To-day it was, from rocky height,
I watched an eagle in its flight;
With soaring circle round and round,
Still rising farther from the ground,
Until fanned the air so high,
'Twas but a speck in cloudless sky;
Nearly 'twere in ether blending,
Pois'd—then like a shot descending.

"I've stood in battle's deadly spot,
Have heard the whizzing hurtling shot,
Have seen the lightning's lurid flash
Hurled 'gainst rock'd wall, with thunder's crash,
But in that eagle's bold descent,
There was power that nature meant;
For only her proud bird of might,
For deadly, falling, striking flight.

"He struck his prey, a panther whelp,
I heard a moaning, piteous yelp,
Then soaring up with graceful ease,
His sight I lost o'er tops of trees.
I thought, brave monarch of the cloud,
How bold art thou, how grandly proud,
No beast on ground, no bird of sky,
Can hide themselves from eagle's eye.

"I had no time for musing more,
An angry wail, a cry, a roar,
A panther dam, all wild with rage,
Not like those cow'd pets in a cage,
But foaming mouth and flashing eye,
Sprang towards me with piercing cry;
I gained my feet, but her hot breath,
Felt in my face like fever'd death.

## THE HUNTER'S CAMP.

" Her fore-arm struck my trusted gun,
Quick from my hand through air it spun;
My rifle useless, now my knife,
Must act the part of life 'gainst life.
It did it well, yes played its part,
She grasped my arm, knife found her heart,
And with a shriek of baffled ire,
Fell at my feet to soon expire.

" That combat lasted but a breath,
In that short time I passed through death,
Yes, passed through death to gain new life,
God bless the man that forged that knife.
I've been in danger's grasp before,
But close as that I want no more.

"That battle o'er I knelt in meekness,
Not for prayer but from weakness;
'Twas a prostrate sinking feeling,
Made me think of early kneeling,
And will own that ere I raised
The Saving Power, thanked and praised.

" There lay my foe, she was the queen
Of all her kind, I've ever seen;
Nine feet from tip to point of nose,
All mottle, like the blue-bush rose.

With muscled arm of might and strength,
And sharpened claws a finger length,
Matchless teeth of ivory white,
Indeed she was a splendid sight.

"I saved her skin, I'll dress it well,
And when I shall the story tell,
Will have the documents to show,
And that's the proof as speakers know.

"I've had enough of Jove's proud bird,
I have my friends, upon my word,
And after this, when eagles fly,
I watch the ground and not the sky.

## OLD MONTE'S BAR FIGHT.

Old Monte sat ready, his lips on the play,
    As could plainly be seen by our glance,
And was only waiting to put in his say,
    If the others would give him a chance.

Zacharias spoke, "Come, old fellow, begin,
    Or the stories won't wind up to-night,
You can have my say, if you'll only sail in,
    Now just give us a whaling bear fight."

"Boys, I belong ter the old fashioned class,
 In all our dealing, went on the squar,
An' war allus willin,' ter lay low an' pass,
 'Cept sich times, as war holden' two par.

"When sharps in the mines got ter using wax cards,
 I own I waxed wroth an' dern'd crusted ;
Why, I got cleaned by my own worthy pards,
 'Till with gamblin' war hugely disgusted.

"I reformed, prefer'd honor to thiev'n,
 An' went in for a game which war far,
So off fur the mountains, found myself leavin',
 Whar I'd go inter dealing for bar.

"But thar ain't no sure thing, on that sort o' game,
 'Tis frequently bad specalation,
Fur they won't never play two hands just the same,
 You can't make a safe calkerlation.

"Bar ar' like people, as ter which thar's no doubt,
 The Brown, Cinnermon, Black an' the Red ;
The one I most hate, ar' the one cleaned me out,
 That old grizzly who left me for dead.

"The difference 'twixt him an' my gambling pards,
 War really no difference at all,
The fust waxed me out by playin' waxed cards,
 The last waxed me out on the call.

"The red bar's an' Injun, with natur the same,
   They're a thieving an' blood-thirsty race,
Neither on 'em haint fit ter be counted game,
   But fur killin' they fill a good place.

"Knockin' a pin from the mishunary cause,
   But you make a good Injun instead,
Thar proper convarsion ter Testermint laws,
   Ar' ter preach 'em the gospel o' lead.

"The Cinnermon bar ar' a ploddin' Chinee,
   Created for somethin' no doubt,
But in all o' my thinkin' have yet ter see,
   Whar that somethin' goes in or comes out.

"I know everything war created fur good,
   From the greatest clean down to the small,
An' this ar' my prayer, 'Oh, Lord that you could
   Keep them critters inside o' thar wall.'

"Unnatralized fill the place o' the brown,
   Don't they stand back, so modestly shy?
But when thar chance 'rives, you bet they come down,
   An' purlitercal fur has ter fly.

"The black bar, of course, he descended from Ham,
   He's the nice petted one o' the lot,
No use ter call him, a snowy fleeced lamb,
   But he haint the wust bar we 'av got.

## THE HUNTER'S CAMP. 69

"The last ar' the grizzly, big boss o' the patch,
   American, Dutch an' Irish combined,
Fur clean fightin' the Old World can't show his match
   When he squarely gits fight on his mind.

"Why, he'll fight anything that ever wore har,
   An'll come ter the scratch every time;
If any you fellers hunts fur grizzly bar,
   You'd better larn fust how ter climb.

"Jist like the American people he ar',
   They haint much on the growl, but a muss,
If any old nation will wake up the bar,
   They'll find him a troublesome cuss.

"So they'd better stand back an' let him alone,
   If they don't, I'll go my last dollar,
That afore they git through with the fight will own,
   He's big dog, what wars the brass collar.

"If you go for a grizzly never try bluff,
   That ar' a game what he wont understand,
You must play him clean out, give him enough,
   If you don't he will sure call your hand.

"If he does make a call, it's two chances in three,
   That he lays you clean out on the shelf,
One o' the chances ar' ter git up a tree,
   An' the other I tried on myself.

" When I fust struck his trail, warnt exactly sure
    Whether he was a grizzly or red,
But found in the end he war infernal pure,
    Yes, a reg'lar old thorough-bred.

" 'Twar an ugly old track, an' heavy behind,
    Sinkin' wus nor an ox in the ground,
The same old feller I'd been wantin' ter find,
    He had long been pirootin' around.

" Sometimes I'd hang up a deer for a change,
    You know it's best way in cool weather,
Steal ? He an' I war dead pints at long range,
    An' now we war comin' tergether.

" He soon left the ridge, turnin' down ter the right,
    Makin' for a little swamp thicket,
I know'd 'twar chance for a grizzly bar fight,
    An' thought ' I'll go in fur a ticket.'

" But it warn't no good place, ter foller him thar,
    Fur his track it war almoughty fresh,
I 'gan ter loose relish, fur that sort o' bar,
    Boys, they hanker too much arter flesh.

" I war goin' around to look at back ways,
    An' slippin' about like as prowlin',
When somebody's har all at once 'gan ter raise,
    Thar he stood, the old feller, growlin'.

"Oh, then fur a tree, but no tree war in sight,
    Nary one could I see round the place,
So then I war in for a grizzly bar fight,
    Squarly up ter the music must face.

"He warn't furder off nor five steps, that war all,
    When he riz up, an' kept gittin' taller,
In my own estermation I war dern small,
    An' all o' the time growin' smaller.

" I knowed I hadn't more nor one chance in ten,
    An' that chance war a sure tellin' shot,
Makin' my prayers, which war short 'jist amen,'
    My bullet crashed home ter the spot.

"I once in my life heard an earthquake afore,
    They cause sorter sick, gaspin' feelin',
It war comin' agin, I heard the same roar,
    Now bar an' not natur wur dealin'.

" An' that's all what I know about that bar fight,
    Fur my eyes war filled full o' smoke,
When my old gun war knocked clean out o' sight,
    An' all on my bones appeared broke.

"The old feller gin me a grizzly bar lick,
    It war lightnin', fur I seed the flash,
Called down my hand an' raked in the trick,
    An' near about settled my 'hash.'

"That blow did me good, cleanin' out my fool sense,
  An' the balance it left moughty small,
All scattered around like the crack o' fence,
  About leaving no idears at all.

" I layed thar still, lettin' things take thar course,
  With courage run down moughty sheep-like ;
As my brain wouldn't work, cause didn't have force,
  'Gan ter gap an' go off sorter sleep-like.

" The old grizzly rolled me this way an' that,
  Then that way an' this 'un instead,
Would stop ter examine, then give me a spat,
  Jist ter see if I really war dead.

" I war moughty glad when he gin up the game,
  Crawlin' off, he laid down with a moan,
I'd liked very well to have did the same,
  'Twould have been sich relief jist ter groan.

" My brains 'gan ter thicken, went off in a dream,
  I had gone to a bare, barren land,
Whar skeleton bars did everywhar gleam,
  Barely able ter walk or ter stand.

" Soon them skeletons turned into human mould,
  With sunken glazed eyes in thar head,
Each came and touched me with fingers so cold,
  'Twar the touch what you feel from the dead.

"Voices war round as in old fashioned days,
  An' the old game war goin' once more,
'Let's see him, an' give him a jolly good raise,'
  Then thar voices sunk lower an' lower.

"A new form had taken his seat at the board,
  Single-handed would play agenst all,
An' that war the reason thar voices lowered,
  He raked every pot on the call.

His features war deathly, not human nor bar,
  With eyes shootin' fire from each socket,
A slimy, scaled coat, all loosely did war,
  With skulls gappin' out o' each pocket.

"I knew who he war without asking his name,
  An' my past deeds smote me in fright;
Oh, how I did hope they'd break up the game,
  'Fore he'd call 'em clean down ter a sight.

"He coaxed 'em, play on, thar lives fur a stake,
  An' the game bein' made it war 'roll,'
The black turned up, the dry bones 'ganter shake,
  As the devil raked in every soul.

"Again the scene changed, I war home in bed,
  Had returned from a long, tired chase,
The maid of my youth standing close by my head,
  An' war soothingly kissing my face.

"I awoke with a start, an' openin' my eyes,
　It war dark an' the moon had riz high,
The bright stars war twinklin' all over the skies,
　In joy I 'most uttered a cry.

" Fur my good faithful dog war close by my side
　Lickin' my face an' fondlin' round me,
As much as ter say, or speak it he tried,
　'Ain't I glad old fellow, I've found ye.'

"That mornin' I told him to stay at the camp,
　Know'd very well he'd mind me,
But at dark when I didn't return from my tramp,
　Old dog-ee had come out ter find me.

" I war nearly gone up, scarcely able ter stand,
　Attempted ter walk but fell sprawlin',
As my legs wouldn't go, jist took it by hand,
　Ter a dry lot o' brush went crawlin'.

"Thar startin' a fire, I thawed myself out,
　An' rubbin' my jints quite bizzily,
By mornin' war able ter be walkin' about,
　Ter look fur my gun an' old grizzly ;

" An' found 'em lyin' no great ways apart,
　The bar fully as cold as the gun,
Had 'parently died from disease o' the heart,
　Like as many another has done.

"As ter his size or his weight I didn't much car,
   Entirely too used up an' sore,
To scarcely look toward that old grizzly bar,
   An' I hope I shan't look at no more.

"If any you fellers wish sport that is rare,
   An' ar in fur a straight out ticket,
You kin git all you want from a grizzly bar,
   If you'll foller him inter a thicket."

## AZTEC MAIDEN.[1]

Far in central Arizona,
O'er a country rough and stony,
  Is hidden a sweet valley,
  A pretty little valley,
  A lovely meadow valley;
Shut in by arid mountains,
There are no springs or fountains,
  But a cool, flowing river,
  A sparkling, glowing river,
  An ever going river—
Gave by the giving Giver,
Was that ever living river
  To a people long departed,
  As 'twere all broken-hearted,
  But living many an art had,
Now gone and lost forever,
To be found out never, never.

But still lingers there a spirit,
That shall guard and e'er stay near it,
  Till is heard the angel warning,
  On the morning of that morning,
  When a new earth all adorning.

Shall own that time's no more.
When from that river shore
　Shall 'rise no fear raid[2] people,
　Shall 'rise no old staid people,
　But shall rise a new made people.
A people to inherit
The land held by their spirit,
　The land where a new birth is,
　The land where a new earth is,
　The land where angel mirth is,
To continue on forever
And be lost again, no, never.

———

We camped in that valley once on a time
　When were searching for diamonds and gold ;
Tarried for weeks to worship sublime,
　And to visit those ruins untold.
No humanity in it were dwelling.
　Not a pale-face had ever been there ;
Yet it seemed as if something was telling
　About voices and breath in the air.

True, the industrious beaver was near,
　His works and houses we everywhere found,
So human-like, that did almost appear
　As though people were yet all around.

Whoever's seen what that animal does
    While toiling from season to season,
Must own there's a point not very obtuse, —
    That point between instinct and reason.

In that lowly vale no Apache dare tread,
    He is fearful, yes fearful of giving
Any insult to the heroic dead,
    Whom he durst not molest while living.
His trails lead around in many long ways,
    Over Mésa,[3] thro' rough cactus thicket,
He'll travel for nights and shun it for days,
    Fearing a "hail" from the lost pickets.

We've hatred against that wild roving thief,
    A hatred that's deep and well founded,
But must respect superstition's belief,
    On all sides with which he's surrounded.
'Twas in that land lovely, that we beheld
    Something that spoke heart's intuition,
Akin to religion, a feeling that swelled
    In us, almost a superstition.

In time long ago that country was filled
    With laboring, dense population,
The earth brought its fruit, each foot being tilled
    By works of complete irrigation.

Castles and dwelling stand yet on the hills,
    All guarded each way by bold tower,
There too they had furnaces, forges and mills
    Which ran by some wonderful power.

---

    'Twas there some new surprise,
    Would meet our wond'ring eyes,
Here a shaft or a column of granite,
    Worked true to the line,
    With its finish so fine,
Causing artistic feelings to scan it.

    Strewn all o'er hill and plain,
    And there long to remain,
For the reading of on-coming ages,
    Were ruins abounding,
    Both grand and astounding,
Which yet shall be pictur'd on pages,

    By some artistic hand
    Who may chance in that land,
That weird land of old sight-seeing splendor,
    Or in some bold verses
    As the poet rehearses
The thoughts that their sights will engender.

The mountains themselves are all hollow'd out
    Into room-ways for mile upon mile,
So the explorer must care what he is about,
    Or is lost in the underground wild.
A band of four men to search those rooms thro',
    We entered and kept moving on,
In hopes to find something or other 'twas new,
    To remind of those who are gone.

Everything in there is just the same,
    The same as it were with the living,
And could we but tell each characters name,
    What mystical tale would be given.
No moisture or mould doth there ever gather,
    'Tis the pole of the great Arid Zone,
The smallest motes and tiniest feather,
    Remain there as left by the gone.

    So we traveled on in wonder,
    Farther in and farther under,
      How far we thus were going
      None thought or cared the knowing,
      While something new was showing,
    Of the many curious things
    Of quaint pottery and rings,
      Of relics and the traces,
      Of the lost forgotten races,
      That we found in those weird places.

Around those rocks so hoary,
What is the written story ?
  Were those characters in mastic,
  Made while the walls were plastic
  By ancient living Aztec ?
Did they write in meaning hidden ?
Yes, to us, 'tis all forbidden.

If we by patient gleaning,
Can but find their storied meaning,
  We will search them to their ending,
  Whether upward or descending,
  However far extending.
A new room that we entered,
Our eyes at once were centered
  On a pictured flying dart,
  Pointing toward a naked heart,
  Whence life drops seem'd to start
From that painted cabalistic,
So mysteriously mystic.

All pointed towards a portal,
As if 'twould say, "No mortal
  Can ever enter herein,"
  But soon we made a clearing,
  And another room were nearing.

There it was, a round, arched chamber,
All lined with glittering amber,
  And right within the fore-way,
  Just apast the door-way,
  There was as plain as mid-day,
A lovely, kneeling maiden,
With gems and jewels laden ;
  While a radiance of splendor,
  Encircled to defend her,
  In a halo that did blend her
Like a holy, fairy spirit,
That might vanish if you'd near it.


We all stood still and spell-bound,
As tho', with cords, were well bound,
  While hearts near ceased their beating,
  None forward or retreating,
  Earth's shadows were completing,
For us a fairy vision,
To the fields of bright Elysian,
  A picture ne'er yet painted,
  In Angelo's saints so sainted,
  They're all by earth so tainted ;
No art hath yet, nor never
Can paint her look forever.

Art is but an ideality,
While there was a reality,
Mortal, immortality ;
The beginning and the ending,
Present and future blending.

She knelt beside pedestal,
Like near the throne celestial,
On floor all laid in moulden,
With devices strangely olden,
Cubed and squared like golden.
Thence from an odor breath-like,
Stole round us still and death-like,
Not death's cold breath all clammy,
But gentle, soothing, balmy,
To ask the question, "am I
In hereafter, or still here?"
When room-way echo answered, "Near."

Her eyes straight to us gazing,
With right hand slightly raising,
Whilst left was falling faintly
Over bosom fair and saintly,
From whence a raiment quaintly
Fell flowing from the waist,
In neatness classic, chaste,

Fell round where she was kneeling,
Like a white robed virgin sealing
A vow there's no repealing,
But each moment growing stronger,
Till earthly time's no longer.

Her hair was soft and flaxen,
Not like the Anglo Saxon ;
  'Twas flossy all and wild-like,
  'Twas mossy, yet tho' mild-like,
  So glossy and so child-like,
Over shoulder it was flowing,
Round a face life-like and glowing,
  Till as a soothing lover
  Did over bosom hover,
  To form a peerless cover.
'Twas no picture of ideal,
We saw and knew 'twas real.

Her lips were slightly parted,
With look, lorn lonely hearted,
  That said as plain as speaking:
  "Seek no farther in your seeking,
  But leave me as a beacon
For my returning nation
In their spiritual creation,

Who in their earthly fading,
Left behind one Aztec Maiden
To guard their land 'gainst raiding
Of the murderous mountain scourge,
Who watched us from each gorge,
But never dared to rally
His allies for a sally
But once, into our valley."


"Then came as a wolf, to lap our heart's blood,
Thief-like, prowled as morning was breaking,
From sleep of the night we scarcely were waken,
Ere he poured in his hordes as a flood.
In stream deep and wide,
Down from mountain's side,
By tramp of his feet our valley was shaken.


"'Twas not for vengeance, he'd suffered no wrong,
But for pillage, and cursed love for slaughter,
To see our life's blood flowing like water,
To lay waste a land where peace sang her song,
Where ties told each other,
That man was a brother,
And woman was sister, wife, or a mother.

" Dire was that morning, and fear hovered round us,
   Bright loving cheeks were blanching and paling,
   From home of the peaceful loud rose the wailing,
The dread scourge of nations had found us.
     That dawn had come quickly
     With scenes sad and sickly,
   My people in terror and agony quailing.


"Some up to their castles hurriedly fled,
   Where they were safe from death's bloody dealing,
   But who could stay there with kindred feeling,
Beholding the many below with the dead ?
     Scarce offering resistance,
     Imploring assistance,
   Sadly pitiful in their appealing.


" There death was busy e'en round their hearth stones,
   The child and mother were falling as one,
   The shriek of the loved ones gave back dying moans,
And blood in our river beginning to run.
Clad as you see me, and armed but with love,
   Quickly I flew from castle to valley,
Claimed for my mission as sent from above,
   Called on my people to rally, to rally.

"Fast from each hillside rushed father and son,
   Old men from castles, young men from the plain,
Rallied together and rallied as one—
   While terror struck boys arose up from the grain,
Each ready and eager to join in the fray.
   So peaceful we'd lived, ne'er been annoyed,
It was hard to look on the blood of that day,
   But it was fight or else be destroyed.

"Fast all round flew our death dealing arrows,
   Sharp was the twang of the string from each bow,
Speaking dire vengeance against morning sorrows,
   Our river grew dark in deep crimson flow.
Our young men embolden'd discarded all fears,
   Advancing with darts as a moving flood,
While old men more steady, with bright gleaming spears,
   Which were soon dyed in avenging blood.

"Soon scales of the battle turned for the right,
   And our foes being everywhere pressed,
Were attempting to gain the mountains in flight,
   But by our warriors were given no rest.
Every pass being held by arrows and spears,
   While deadly hatred was standing behind,
Those craven-souled brutes who fell in their fears,
   Whipped wolves, eating dust as they whined.

"Whined for their lives, but no sympathy found,
    That was forfeited in seeking ours,
So with strongest cords we had them all bound,
    And led them safe to high guarded towers.
There they were given into hands of the priests,
    To be sacrificed, many each day,
Their flesh for the ravens, the vultures and beasts,
    Thus for the crime of their raiding to pay.

"The ravens embolden'd from eating such food,
    From the mountains swarmed round every side,
And vultures came many, with mates and their brood,
    But proud eagle stood back in his pride.
To feed that noble bird the priests did prepare,
    Huge granite blocks to fasten the living,
That he might pounce down on his part of the fare,
    Helping to mete out the punishment given.

"The hordes watched from far and saw them dying,
    Saw wolves licking bones with quarrelsome yelp,
Saw bird of the air with carrion flying,
    While standing aghast, not daring to help.
Thus moons came and went till their punishment passed,
    But our foes ne'er again came around,
The cries of their kindred they heard on night's blast,
    To their fears every breath bringing sound."

"Since that morning long years and cycles have rolled,
  Montezuma called my people away,
  They departed to come at some future day,
But crowned and left me their spirit, to hold,
    This land of dear yearning,
    Until their returning,
  Which they shall behold in spirit or clay.


" Well, I've defended our homes since they left,
  Night coming on with dark shadows stealing.
  Garbed as I am, I raise from my kneeling,
And walk the night air from some hidden cleft,
    In spirit and power,
    Sounding note from high tower,
  All o'er the valley, the echoes pealing.


"Our foes hear and tremble in dreadest affright,
  The past lesson had import so fearful,
  Even till now their eyes gather tearful,
When still hearing cries of their kindred at night,
    All suffering, anguished
    On tower where they languished
  In wailing tones, as something past drearful.

"Thus have I guarded, and thus shall I hold,
Until on-coming ages relieve me ;
You, a new race, I know you believe me ;
Let me remain in my crowning of gold
    Till that high word is spoken
    No more to be broken ;
'Faithful spirit, time ends to reprieve thee.'

"I know you'll not touch any jewel or band,
That's adorning my bosom, armlet or hand,
  But leave me chaste, as fair as you found me,
  Nothing displaced from glory around me,
  Spirit life graced, as the day they crowned me,
And each take with you maiden's love,
As pure as breath, of All Above."

    I turned to leave, but not alone,
    Each comrade near were bringing stone ;
    No word was spoke, but thoughts the same,
    From each one went, to each one came.
    We walled that passage o'er and well,
    So that no others e'er can tell ;
    Within that lonely hiding place,
    Is last of Montezuma's race.

No one had thought, no one did bring,
To light of day a hidden thing;
We left them all within those rooms,
They were not ours, they were the tombs'.
'Tis true they'd add a page to history,
In clearing up a long lost mystery,
Of which we now have scarce a trace,
Of that almost forgotten race.

But who that hath a manly feeling,
Would snatch a form so lovely, kneeling?
If there be such, he'd rob a chapel,
Or give his loved one to the scalpel.
Who would that "lost one" desecrate,
Would rob your coffin of its plate,
And steal pure virtue, fair enshrin'd;
To mock at woe he'd left behind.

No, right is right, and wrong is wrong,
The weak hath power against the strong,
That power of conscious innate might
That bids us all uphold the right.
Uphold it you, where'er you can,
Such acts and deeds makes man a man.

## EXPLANATORY NOTES TO AZTEC MAIDEN.

1 Those who have traveled over northern Sonora, or central Arizona, more especially the head waters of the Gila, Salt River, or Rio Verde, have noticed the many ancient ruins, scattered far and wide through a country wild, dangerous, picturesque and dreary. Wild from scarcely having been explored, dangerous from the ever hostile Apache, picturesque from its visioned aridness, and dreary from that continued longing lonesome feeling that mankind ever have when among ruins whose builders once were, but now are no more. Among those many and old labyrinths, catacombs, and ruins, of which we speak, is much food for the thoughtful and inquiry for the archeologist. Around and on all sides are signs of an advanced civilization, but by what race or nation there is no certainty. Were they Toltecs? Were they Aztecs? All we know from history ; all we can learn from the traditions of the Pimas or other Pueblo Indians, is the single word " Montezuma," and that the builders are gone—gone.

2 All the ancient dwellings appear to have been built not only for home and hearth, but also for defense, showing that the Apaches or Bedouins, of Arizona, are the descendants of robbers from time immemorial ; and there is no doubt but the "lost inhabitants," who are now no more, were as fearful of his "raids" or attacks, as the moderns have been.

3 Mesa—(Pronounced Ma-sa) Spanish, table. Usual signification, table-land, or high, level plain.

# CASTLE DOME; OR, THE GOLD KING.

Far beyond the Desert's sands,
In fabled diamond lands,
There a wondrous mountain stands,
   That towering Castle Dome.
'Tis about that mountain old,
Many stories you'll be told,
How the shining king of gold,
   Has that castle for his home.
You see it from each highland,
   You behold it from the plain,
'Tis like a signal island,
   For the sailors on the main,
A land-mark for those regions,
   With outlines bold and grand,
And many are the legends
   You'll hear in that wild land,
About that weird old mountain,
   With sombre clouded shadow,
That pictured Castle Dome,
   Of Rio Colorado.

In fiction's fields so fairy,
I've built my castles airy,
Till mind refused to carry,
　The imagings it wrought,
And the wildly running brain
Had forged an endless chain,
With no ending in the train
　Of its ever grasping thought.
Then halting, I have pondered
　Of the fancies of the mind,
Till the spirit wandered,
　Seeking spirits of its kind,
Unto that shadowy distance
　That oftimes is so seeming,
As 'twere a new existence
　We fancy in our dreaming;
When earthly toils and sorrows
　Are still on the river's side,
But the soul hath glimpses over,
　To white shore beyond the tide.

But in the wildest soaring in romantic fiction's field
    Mind had never figured what mine eyes did behold,
'Neath that castelated Dome where earth herself had sealed,
    The home of her great king, the Royal King of Gold.
It was far across the desert, where the Colorado
    Moves its turbid waters, o'er winding beds of sand,
Where that isolated mountain, with sombre clouded shadow,
    Stands a spectral goblin, to guard the desert land,
Beneath that vaulted temple is the Gold King's golden home,
His wealth, his court, his splendor, are within that Castle Dome.

I'd traveled many weary miles, o'er sandy deserts wide,
    Had crossed yawning chasms, each pathway but a span,
And pierced the vaults of nature, where she had strove to hide
    Her golden mysteries, from searching eyes of man.
Had scaled lofty mountains, where 'twould almost take the breath,
    To view the fissures of convulsions old and grand,
Where to make a mis-step, would be courting kingly death,
    Who is ever standing with grasping, bony hand.
Thus moving like a spirit that can never cease to roam,
Till at the shades of even was camped 'neath Castle Dome.

In the west, o'er sandy plain, the sun was sinking fast,
  While Nature lay reposing on white riffs of sand,
When from far across the desert, there came a moving blast,
  With a cadence onward, towards the mountain land.
'Twere like a waking nation with one endless marching tread,
  When marshalling its armies, a fight for life or death,
Or as the Judgment Trumpet had 'wakened up the dead,
  And all inanimation transformed to living breath.
'Twas swelling like an ocean, when storm-lashed into foam,
  While on moved a living army towards the Castle Dome.

No order there existed, not a vanguard for the van,
  None smiled on other, but all like glaring foes,
Dashed along the mountain to out-strip their fellow man,
  And win the golden castle before its gates would close.
Like giant trees of forest madly writhing 'mid the storm,
  Or the sands of desert when the simoom is loud,
This human, wild tornado, only human-like in form,
  Was streaming onward along the mountain road.
It was a wild, weird pageant, that in awe I did behold,
The massing of an army 'gainst the shining King of Gold.

## CASTLE DOME.

When it burst on my vision, I strove a while to think,
'Twas some imagination, or chimera of the brain,
And should I but go to it, like dreaming spell 'twould sink,
Leaving me all lonely, in my lone camp on the plain.
Then up towards the Castle Dome, was in the seething flood,
That was beating onward, a river deep and wide,
Oh no, 'twas no illusion, they all were flesh and blood,
In stream resistless, as the ever flowing tide;
While I was fleetly borne along, a floating speck at most,
A drifting leaf, upon Time's tide, and moving with the host.

'Twas Babel of confusion, every nation, every tongue,
Pressing on together in maddened, flowing stream,
Old age infirmly haggard, vied with the daring young,
While light from sunken eyes in fitful flash would gleam.
There was the sharpened Yankee around on every side,
Who strove with all his craft to win the golden race,
But his natural cunning was balked or sorely tried,
By the sons of Jewry, who kept their dog-trot pace.
They seemed to know each by-path, as hungry curs their home,
While others gained no entrance, these entered Castle Dome.

We passed beneath the archway of lofty, massive gates,
  Into a court yard, where gold banners were unfurled;
'Twas so large 'twould hold the conclave of kingdoms and of states
  In mass convention, to reorganize a world.
With walls of height and distances, in width out-reaching plain,
  In length, past conception; drawn out to endless length,
From terminus of vision you could look and look again,
  And never see their ending; vision hath not strength
To penetrate one tithe the distance o'er which the King of Gold
  Sways sceptre of dominion, as beneath this mountain old.

Standing within the court yard was a hall of vast extent,
  Where Nature's architect had shown her perfect law,
In proportions composite, it was altogether blent,
  As pleasing to the eye, as filling mind with awe.
There wisdom, strength and beauty, were equally combined,
  With matchless symmetry in their various parts,
The finish was perfection geometrical aligned,
  Out vieing all buildings e'er built by human arts.
Not the world's praised arching o'er St. Peter's Church at Rome
  Can equal that grand canopy o'er-hanging Castle Dome.

Tho' we were in the court-yard, none had gained the hall
    Where Gold King held levies, disbursing bounties rare,
But with a shouting clamor, 'twas forward one and all,
    And then there was crowding as to a nation's Fair.
But none gained an entrance, each door was guarded well,
    By a Stone-Faced Knight, who with heavy lance and mace,
Dealt valiant blows full thick and fast, and many by him fell,
    Yet like the dragon's teeth, men rose to fill each place.
Soon Stone-Face Knight was bleeding, full sore from every vein,
    Which raised a shouting clamor, "Up and at him once again."

The gates gave way before us, we gained the Golden Hall,
    Where Gold King was throned in golden chair of state;
While scarcely thought was given for the many that did fall,
    By the vanquished knight, who defended every gate.
They fell not in cause of country, but struggling for gold,
    Each and all forgotten, in turmoil, as they fell,
Belonging to Death's army, where names are not enrolled,
    Save in earth's last discharge, 'tis there they're written well.
Thus perished many legions, who'd fallen in the fight,
Around the walls of Castle Dome, by Gold King's deadly knight.

Who was that valiant warrior, that stalwart Stone-Faced
    Knight,
  Bravely defending each passage to the castle?
With tried arms of adamant, and armor snowy white,
  Ever doing service as the Gold King's vassal.
Like the fabled spirit Brocken, on mountain of Schwartz,
  He's a standing giant and pillar of the earth,
And is known throughout the world as gold bearing
    Knightly Quartz,
  The guardsman of gold treasure since creation's birth;
And whoever wins the castle where Gold King lives and
    reigns,
  Must battle with Sir Flinty Quartz, 'till he bleeds at many
    veins.

In his great crystal body they'll find a mighty giant,
  Resisting every blow and grasping close his treasure,
Only under strength and might is he to be made pliant,
  Owning man is worthy a lance with him to measure,—
This famous golden guardsman, with limbs that gird all land,
  With veins flowing in and arteries shooting out,
Had been found by vast army where he'd made a valiant
    stand,
  Time-being vanquished and his forces put to rout;
At gates where he was guarding Gold King's treasured
    home,
  Within their granite casements deep under Castle Dome.

There is no daylight shining within that spacious hall,
   Tho' we see its grandeur, e'er our eyes are turning,
For there is no settled darkness, nor sombre clouded pall,
   All is brightly glowing as thousand lamps were burning.
Around the vast expansion either to the left or right,
   Shooting up the dome-way as tho' 'twould burst thro' it,
As fiery darting meteors that sometimes 'lume the night,
   With a radiance that pains the eye to view it;
And golden scintillations, like the lightning, as it runs,
And shining with effulgence, as doth the sun of suns.

Those lights so brilliant shining are not the lights of day,
   Neither are reflection from planet, moon or star,
We're so deep within the mountain that not a single ray,
   Of heated glowing sunlight could penetrate thus far.
Then what is that with radiant flame now lighting up the
     Court ?
Showing all the windings within the mountain old,
So brilliantly, that even of sunlight 'twould make sport,
   Disclosing the pockets and crevices of gold.
They are gems, diamonds, brilliants, flaming in grand pyre,
That would dazzle, pale, and darken a planet clothed in fire.

None thought about the grandeur, but coveted the gold,
   Each graceful column tho' reared in beauty's form,
And standing grandly, proudly, as the Pantheon of old,
   Melted as if snow flakes beneath a south wind storm.

For this destroying army, sweeping onward down the hall,
    Like glaciered avalanche, destruction in its path,
Not leaving single bright spot, but blotting out the all,
    As the vales of Gila, by the Apache's wrath,—
Gold King's power was shaken, again arose his vassal,
Lights ceased their shining and blackness clothed the Castle.

As lights gave way to darkness, there 'rose unearthly howls,
    From those who sank under their massive loads of gold,
Night spirits quickly gathered, great vampires and fierce ghouls,
    With breath as poisonous as is the fire-damp mould.
Strong men who dared all danger, whose every limb was health,
    Trembled, weak and falling into the sleep of sleeps,
Buried by the weight of their grasping toil-gained wealth,
    With none to own it, as it lay in golden heaps.
Not one was left living to disclose the Gold King's home,
Not one to tell the mysteries that's hid 'neath Castle Dome.

He that travels o'er the desert of the Colorado,
    Where sandy desolation is moving as the wind,
Where mirages of wonder are floating as a shadow,
    Like an *ignts fatuus*, he'll never, never find.
Will behold that mountain as a land-mark for those lands,
    And from whence he views it, will look and gaze again,
Toward its weird, wild summit, where it proudly stands,
    Like sentinel on duty, to guard each golden vein.
And should he e'er at eve-tide, camp 'neath its shadows bold,
Will hear that tramping army, that is marching on for gold.

# A CENTENNIAL.

## DEDICATION.

To go ahead and put 'er thro'
   Great American nation,
We dedicate our verse to you,
   Not Gospel, nor Salvation;
But in a kinder sorter way,
   A plain historic story,
Simply attempt to have a say
   About our nation's glory.

Written in American tongue,
   In fact we know not other,
We chanced to learn it when quite young,
   Yes, learned it from our mother.
So don't expect an old Greek verse,
   Nor lugged-in Latin phrases,
Our own bold language is as terse,
   And blooming like the daisies.

A language that contains the gold
   Of every living nation,
As far ahead the "dead and old,"
   As we're ahead creation.
The measure is both longs, and shorts,
   Some small and others greater,
In fact you'll find it most all sorts
   To suit our human natur.

The critic may lampoon it some,
   To prove himself a noodle,
But let him beat down, "Hail Colum,"
   Or tramp out "Yankee Doodle,"
When he does that "he'll have to pass,"
   And our's will never heed it,
Because the people as a mass,
   Will sorter like to read it.

# AMERICA.

Of proud America we sing,
    Year of thy centennial birth,
Thou land that's opened freedom's spring
    That yet shall water all the earth ;
Thou land to which thy sons shall cling
    As family to home and hearth ;
And guard thee well until the last,
As they have guarded in the past.

What thoughts to us, an hundred years,
    A cradled child to Freedom born,
The parents of that one no fears,
    Calm christened it, a July morn ;
Christened it with thankful tears,
    Tho' it was held in Royal scorn ;
But Liberty stood near and smiled,
Blessed Freedom's nation, then a child.

The mother of that precious one,
    Had watched the strife at Bunker Hill,
Had seen the fray at Lexington,
    And there resolved with Roman will
That she would bare a noble son,
    Whose very name should one day thrill
A world with gratitude and joy,
That she had borne a priceless boy.

Blessed parents, who in thoughts conceived
    Our precious child of Liberty,
Who in their hopeful hearts believed,
    A land of promise you should see,
A land where none should be aggrieved,
    But all your sons and daughters free;
As free in thought, as free in mind,
A land of hope for all mankind.

An Otis watched his opening breath,
    An Adams spoke, " The child shall live ;"
" For me, this priceless one, or death,"
    A Henry said, "The world shall give."
And kingly power like pale Macbeth,
    Fell cowering back in fear to grieve;
When mother true chose Washington
To be the guardian of her son.

America—new born nation,
 'Thy noblest, brightest names were there,
Pledging honor, life and station,
 By signature and word did swear,
Thou, the last of earth's creation,
 Should be the fairest of the fair;
So fair indeed the world should see,
The new born one was Liberty.

Loud the bell from that old tower,
 Sent news of gladness, fast and wide,
The tottering of old kingly power
 Rolled from our shore, an ebbing tide ;
While each gave thanks, that happy hour,
 For Declaration of our pride;
All men created, equal, free,
With equal rights to Liberty.

The cradled child so small and young,
 Scarce grew at all the first seven years,
But using arms as well as tongue,
 E'en whipped Dame Britain with his tears ;
And mother land from which he sprung,
 Was forced to love him thro' her fears,
And said, "You're English, true and bold,
Independent, seven years old."

To follow thro' that patriot strife,
    Until the child could walk alone,
Those deeds on history's page are rife,
    'Twas in that struggle there was sown
The germs, that opened Freedom's life
    Throughout the world, as despots own,
''Till other nations caught the blaze,
That shall burn on till end of days.

That periled strife, how shall we tell
    Of suffering ones at Valley Forge ?
But in their hearts a fire did dwell,
    To thaw the ice within that gorge,
Till melted did a torrent swell,
    That washed the throne of Old King George,
And let him know an infant born
Would live to hurl such thrones to scorn.

'Twas from that valley Freedom's band
    Moved towards the ice bound Delaware,
Tho' clad in rags their steps were grand,
    'Twas to a world they would declare
Themselves the heroes of a land,
    Who had the hearts to do and dare ;
Bare-footed heroes, on they trod
With trust in Washington and God.

On Trenton's snowy ice-bound field,
    The proud old Lion sleeping lay,
When suddenly his bugles pealed,
    " A rebel band—a little fray."
' Twas Liberty—they had to yield,
    For Freedom was a host that day ;
King George had lost, the child had won.
Praise for that day and Washington.

Not falter, on thro' ice and cold,
    Till wintry Princeton was in view,
From morning fray each heart beat bold,
    While each resolved to die or do;
And like the storm-king, on they rolled,
    Till e'en before proud Britain knew,
Another battle, fought and won,
The child again with Washington.

Thus from his little cradled sleep,
    The boy began to make his way,
Not walking yet, but he could creep,
    And with the crown of king would play,
To make of it a ruined heap,
    Without so much as by your say ;
George beheld in kingly wonder,
Chatham spoke, " You'll hear it thunder."

The King replied, "I'll teach the lad
A lesson that he'll not forget,"
In truth his ministers were glad,
It gave excuse for them to let
Loose such war dogs as they had!
Those acts we most remember yet ;
Their murderous hordes wildly roaming,
Blood from Lakes to "Fair Wyoming."

They loosed upon the distant child,
The power of home with Hessian band,
While each to other gayly smiled,
To see the hosts at their command ;
Besides their Indian allies wild,
But all were met—met hand to hand,
And where they won success to-day,
To-morrow saw it fade away.

Soon poured a stream from northern wilds,
Wild Canadian land,
'Twas met by guardians of the child,
A stalwart yeoman band,
With a hero at their head ;
"Here, boys, we'll make a stand,
And give them lead for lead,

Till proud Britain's host shall own
    For once they've had to yield,
Or Mollie Stark sleeps alone,
    I'll sleep upon the field."

Then cheered the boy, " On heroes, on,
    Your cause is mine, and just,"
And ere sun set, proud Bennington,
    Saw trailing in the dust ;
The olden banners grand,
Of mighty mother land,
Which said her children must
Pay tribute to a kingly throne,
    The tribute that they owe,
But on that day they had to own,
    America said " No."

The tide of battle onward rolled,
    The little one awake,
Huzza'd and shouted loud and bold,
    'Twas heard from hill to lake,
And answered by a shout,
That caused the mountains shake,
Dispelling kingly doubt,
In the head of that old fogy,
    Doing 'way his wonder,
For the news from Saratoga,
    Was the coming thunder.

Those bold deeds did a world inspire,
    And outside nations first to mock
The little child, beheld his fire,
    And heard his Saratoga talk;
The little one was creeping higher,
    When Louis said, "We'll help you walk,
You've won your stars by deeds, not chance,
Shall be upheld by arms of France."

No longer babe, our little lad
    Did doff his dress and mewling cap,
Had tweaked the nose of old king Dad,
    Besides, could give him rap for rap;
And wasn't the little fellow glad,
    That he could do without his "pap,"
A leading friend to take his hand,
Assistance both to walk and stand.

Time moved along, the lad grew bold,
    By play of war game here and there,
Through northern ice and winter cold,
    Oft with his little feet most bare;
But soon the tide of conflict rolled,
    Towards his southern climate fair,
And lo! our little laddie stood,
'Side Marion in the piny wood.

## MARION'S MEN.

The little fellow felt a thrill
    Of high-born childish joys,
His ev'ry pulse and heart veins fill,
    He'd got among his boys.

He shouted long, and shouted loud,
    Till piny woodlands rang,
Oh! wasn't the little hero proud
    To hear the sabres clang.

His partizans were proud as he,
    His orders given then,
A conquering column down Santee,
    With Marion and his men.

'Twas battle here, or charge you there,
    Thro' glade, swamp, or thicket
Till every Britisher did swear,
    They daren't leave a picket.

His Southern blood was warming well,
    Bold Briton's tide to stem,
Full soon they knew, as they could tell,
    That it was warming them.

The little handful, tho' but few,
    Increased from day to day,
While each to little lad were true,
    And had their little say.

Their words were these, "My boy, fight on,
    Tho' long the strife may be,
We'll trust in God and Washington,
    Who says we shall be free."

———

Whatever place the lad would go,
    His brave men on the field
Stood ready each, to meet the foe,
    "We'll die, but never yield."

With Morgan and his riflemen,
    The little hero now
Did make his mark at Old Cowpen,
    He made his mark somehow.

But it was made with sabres keen,
    From arms 'twere stout and strong,
While fast the boy with Quaker Greene,
    Was moving things along.

The tide of war began to flow,
   In straight channels deep and narrow,
The boy was giving blow for blow,
   Keen to-day, sharper to-morrow,
And where a Briton ploughed to sow,
   He followed with the harrow;
Followed so close each Briton found
That kingly power was losing ground.

Cornwallis, last of England's host,
   A lord in blood of royal line,
Who had come over with a boast,
   "When Rebels see a Lord divine,
They will fall in the dust e'en most,
   I'll make them, yes, I'll make them whine,
And ask of me in loyal tone,
That I will intercede the throne."

How was it? In the mighty range
   Of chance, sometimes calculation
Fail. Cornwallis thought very strange,
   To see so little veneration,
And just by way to make a change,
   The Lord found for own salvation,
Instead of hearing, "Lord, forgive,"
The Lord it was who asked to live.

He had learned at bloody cost,
　Lordly boasting was not doing,
A battle won or battle lost,
　Everywhere the boy pursuing,
If perchance a river crossed,
　'Twas to escape impending ruin,
Till with tired force he settled down,
For last defence at old Yorktown.

The boy now learned in arts of war,
　No longer idle was around,
From being dared 'twas he to dare,
　The last defender of the crown;
Calling his forces near and far,
　He'd fight it out before Yorktown:
The Lord beheld his race was run,
The boy was there with Washington.

But we'll pass on towards brighter days,
　Freedom's sun was getting higher,
Full soon the boy would have a say,
　All independent of his sire;
For thro' the world America
　Had kindled an undying fire,
Small at first with Freedom glowing,
But how fast the flame was growing.

To check the flame King George in vain
  Used his means and royal forces,
To rivet fast the fettered chain,
  Had near exhausted all resources;
Kings are mortals, therefore 'tis plain,
  Mortals often change their courses;
George changed his, for simple reason.
Mistook Freedom, called it treason.

Kings sometime can't help the doing,
  Tho' it is strictly 'gainst their creed,
Working towards monarchial ruin,
  To e'en attempt a noble deed;
Old George beheld wild storms were brewing,
  Began to think it best take heed,
If he would save his crown and throne,
The error of his ways must own.

Great Britain dared no longer wait,
  Yorktown confounded, worse confusion,
So George called in his guides of State,
  All arrived at same conclusion,
To fight the boy was fighting fate,
  To conquer worse than delusion.
The verdict was: "Our descendant,
Is both Free and Independent."

## AMERICA.

Our little youth, seven years old,
    Had broke from Britain's chains and bars,
And wrote his name in living gold,
    As bright as any son of Mars;
Besides had grasped to firmly hold,
    His Eagle with her Stripes and Stars;
Emblems of might—Eternity,
And talisman of Liberty.

The boy in war had made his way
    Thro' long years, both dark and drearful,
The sun of peace arose to say,
    Thine eyes no longer to be tearful,
Shall shine as doth the king of day,
    Like her light, be ever cheerful;
Heroes were there, when war should cease,
To guide the youth down paths of peace.

Immortal men, heroes, sages,
    Your works for us, your deeds for fame,
Records for Time's latest pages,
    Where each shall have undying name;
And Liberty thro' coming ages,
    Shall your every actions claim.
While fire you started ne'er shall smoulder,
But burn brighter as grows older.

To speak your names our verse were proud,
　To tell their worth could only try,
There's one at least, who rode the cloud,
　To grasp the lightnings from the sky,
Of whom America's endowed,
　One of her sons not born to die;
Among bright minds that nature blest,
A Franklin stands beside the rest.

---

Those heroes we will not forget;
　Noble patriots, there and then,
Sages, we almost think till yet,
　From us a different race of men,—
Immortal names, 'sides Lafayette,
　When shall we see their like again?
Heaven gave to earth a single son,
Earth to Heaven, a WASHINGTON.

# OSSALINTA.[1]

### PART I.

From the source of Ossalinta,
    Near the mountain's snowy summit,
Over rocks gnarled and flinty,
    Sparkling drops fall like a plummet.

Dancing rainbows come and vanish
    In the sunshine's playful gleaming,
Every care from heart to banish,
    Making day thoughts pleasant dreaming.

Round that spot where beauty lingers,
    In the garb of Nature's giving,
Ne'er disturbed by artful fingers
    On the hand of human living;

There are pretty glades abounding,
    Meadow lawns about it lying,
'Mid dense forest trees surrounding
    With Æolian breath-like sighing.

From each white rock ever springing,
    Little rivulets meander,
While sweet lullabys are singing;
    Nilsson's voice was never grander.

Soon they're joining songs together,
　　Where their waters all are meeting,
Dimple spray-like, floating feather,
　　Crystal drops they are completing.

On adown the cañon falling
　　Over rocks they never mind it,
Where each drop's forever calling,
　　To the spray it left behind it.

Yes, adown its pathway roaring,
　　Toward Hoopa Reservation,
Foaming waters, falling, pouring,
　　With their wild reverberation.

Soon to make their last descending
　　In ether west so glowing,
Where each sunlit ray is blending
　　With the waters ever flowing.

Like the play spot of their starting
　　Over rock gnarled and flinty,
Now their echoes are departing,
　　Past the Falls of Ossalinta.

And its waters pure and sparkling,
　　Like youth from homeland going,
In that muddy river's darkling,[2]
　　As it were life's tide that's flowing.

## PART II.

Below these falls in cañon gray,
   A little nook is lying,
Beyond the reach of falling spray,
   That's round it ever flying.

Shut in by bending scrubby oaks,
   'Most hid by mossy rock-way,
Just move a branch that entrance chokes,
   You stand within a lock-way.

There it is, a grotto bower,
   'Twas Nature's art that made it,
She did it with her spray drop power,
   As on the rocks she played it.

None scarce would notice it around,
   A hidden, cave like wonder,
The water's echoes giving sound,
   Not like their outward thunder;

But in a sad and mournful tone
   Are wailing thro' the bower,
Perhaps it is the dying moan,
   Of little Pale-Flower.[3]

Who was she? That we cannot tell,
   Those rocks refuse the story,
The deed was done within that dell,
   The place was once all gory.

Tradition says her face was fair,
    And that her locks were golden,
Some tiny threads of silken hair
    Are yet 'neath moss rock olden.

She came from toward the rising sun,
    A captive lone and lonely,
Of kith and kin, she here had none,
    All slain, they saved two only.

Saved them for a fate 'twas worse,
    For savage lust and pleasure,
That passion that is mankind's curse,
    Below the beasts 'twill measure.

She had been one of moving train
    That came from some far region,
Of hundred, all save two were slain,
    So sayeth storied legend.

One of the two was kept a slave,
    In eastern Modoc vallies,
The other by consent they gave
    To western mountain allies.

(Now here she was with this cursed band,)
    A thing of bartered trading,
A floweret from some sunny land,
    This once fair little maiden.

What was she now? A thing at best,
    Made so by savage dealing,
Scarce was there left within her breast,
    A ray of woman feeling.

So had been used in savage ways,
    By lovers dark and swathy,
These heroes of an hundred "lays"
    In works like Hiawatha.

This race that need forever get
    A share of christian teaching,
But where's the one that's ever yet
    Been better made by preaching?

We spend our breath, we give our blood,
    With health and monied prizes,
But where are those that learneth good,
    Ere learning all our vices.

Go preach to tiger in his lair;
    'Twould be gospel perversion,
But soon I'd think, true fruits 'twould bear,
    As Indian pure conversion.

Their leading passions are but two,
    One is fearing, 'other's hate,
To work on these that's what's to do,
    By missioned Church or State.

First make him fear, then weed out hate,
  Ere changing his condition,
The first belongs to powers o' State,
  Then go forth with your mission.

And when you shall work change of heart,
  In tribe of these vile curses,
Then we will take the Quaker part,
  Extol it in our verses.

But we will back to rocky bower,
  Our little tale pursuing,
And speak o' Pale-Face, little flower,
  Now but a little ruin.

A throng of braves, God 'fend the name,
  Painted faced and sooty,
Were playing to see which should claim
  The little fading beauty.

They played and won her, time again,
  Till each had passion sated,
'Twere better far had she been slain,
  With kindred bloody fated.

Now she was dying in this place,
  With body torn and bleeding,
Surrounded by chival'rous race
  Known of in novel reading.

With parched lips and fever'd brow,
  None to relieve her anguish,
Oh, could the angels take her now,
  Nor let her longer languish.

But no, she was the White man's race,
  An object of their hating,
A smile came o'er each savage face,
  For further torture sating.

With sharpened knife, one clove an ear,
  Another clove a finger,
The blood still ran to raise a cheer,
  " Her sufferings would linger."

Now piece by piece, and limb by limb,
  In demon laugh's derision,
And that her eyes should have no film,
  At each new flesh incision,

They were removed with savage grin,
  Torn forth from sunken socket,
While scarcely life was left within,
  Save in its heart beat locked.

All quickly tore her frail breast part,
  The last dire act completing,
The strings that held her little heart,
  Had severed its last beating.

## PART III.

Yet to those Falls will Red man come,
    With boat from lower river,
But there for time his voice is dumb,
    His hardened frame will shiver.

And tremble like the alder leaf,
    O'er boiling waters bending,
It is not vengeance, neither grief,
    With their emotions lending.

He's fearful of Pale Face power,
    Their might has had a trial,
Fears that yet, that rocky bower
    May pour its wrathful vial.

And so it will if ever hate
    Should raise above his fearing,
There shall be arms 'sides those of State,[4]
    That then will have a hearing.

# EXPLANATORY NOTES TO OSSALINTA.

[1] Ossalinta is a small river, some twenty miles in length, formed from the melting snow and innumerable springs of the summit range, and flows into the Trinity river at the Falls of Ossalinta, a few miles above the Hoopa Reservation. The scenery, at the falls and to its very source, is as grand as can be found in any part of California ; and till yet, few, if any, white men have penetrated its wilds—yes, WILDS.

[2] The Trinity, like nearly all our mountain rivers, is a mining stream, and at points where a clear river or creek empties, the waters run but a short distance, until, like a youth in bad company, the commingling waters are soon all of same color.

[3] The following, taken from an Oregon paper, will explain itself :

"In the year 1852, while an emigrant train was on the way to the southern portion of Oregon, it was attacked by a band of hostile Modocs. The train numbered nearly one hundred souls, all of whom were massacred except two young girls, sisters, aged about fourteen and sixteen, who were taken prisoners. To the right of the road leading from Small's and Van Bremer's ranches, and within a short distance of Dorris' house, there is a big ledge of rocks that overlooks to the north a narrow valley stretching away towards Little Klamath Lake. Here, when savage jealousy had made her an object of contention, or when her ruined body could no longer administer to savage lust, the elder sister was murdered. The younger had died previously, but under what circumstances is not known."

[4] Written during time of an Indian panic, when each miner and settler were willing to take a hand against the expected outbreak.

# THE "LOST ONE" OF SAN JUAN.

There's many an old Mission,
  Built in ancient times,
Adown our southern coast range
  In orange growing climes.

And many a quaint old story
  That you will hear of each,
How faithful, loving Padres,
  Could love as well as preach.

I'll tell one of those stories,
  'Tis but a little lay,
And happened ere the glory
  Of Missions passed away.

It had a loving Padre,
  Who loved his children well,
And when he left the Mission,
  Left witnesses to tell

A plain and homely story,
  That hath one truth at least,
It is not every Padre
  Who is a holy priest.

That time old church was standing,
  Its walls as white as snow,
The pride of lovely Mission,
  In years of 'long ago.'

But now its lonesome ruins,
  Only speak of past and gone,
How it fell to save a pure soul,
  The "Lost One" of San Juan.

Of hundred dark eyed maidens,
  The very words they told;
"One was the purest diamond,
  Tho' all the rest were gold."

Juanita, lost Juanita,
  Fairest flower of all,
That evening 'tended vespers
  At Holy Fathers' call;

And tarried at confession
  Till all the rest were gone,
Since then no eye hath seen her
  The "Lost One" of San Juan.

From that Old Mission's legends,
  They tell you on that night,
The earth it rose and trembled
  All saw a golden light

And heard an angel singing,
    A song of sweetest love,
Each thought their good old Padre,
    Had soar'd to realms above.

Those pious, rural people,
    In awe beheld the sight,
Hurrying to the old church
    With an increasing fright;

Instead of house of refuge
    Beheld a ruined heap,
And they without a shepherd,
    Like lost, forsaken sheep.

Each knelt about the ruins,
    To say a holy prayer,
The vaquero and peon
    'Side Señoritas fair.

Thus they passed the night through,
    Until the morning dawn,
That night of desolation
    At Mission of San Juan.

Just at the morning's breaking,
    Their loving Padre found
His crime was known in heaven,
    His blood was on the ground.

When eyes he slowly opened,
   All knelt expecting prayer,
To only hear deep curses,
   "You're mine, you're mine, I swear"—

"Call to your Holy Mother,
   I've barred the doors full well,
You have no help from heaven—
   Great God, the walls have fell;

"Juanita; where's Juanita?"
   His struggling breath was gone,
While last words ne'er were answered,
   At Mission of San Juan.

---

I wandered 'neath those ruins,
   By pale and mellow light,
Of full moon in her glory,
   A California night.

Of full moon in her glory,
   When filleth crystal air
With countless floating ringlets
   Of silver sheeny hair.

When more you view her splendor,
  The more you seeming try
To penetrate that future
  Beyond the moonlit sky.

Such was the night all lovely,
  Its hours were flying fast,
And lonely I sat musing,
  About the gone and past.

I saw the old church standing,
  As in the time that's gone,
And saw those ancient people,
  Then living at San Juan.

With hundred dark eyed maidens
  Grouped on the plaza's lawn
And among them fair Juanita,
  The "Lost One" of San Juan.

I knew her in a moment,
  Her sylph like form so fair
Moved like a floating zephyr
  That threads the lightest air.

Who's seen fair Spanish maiden,
  Can e'er forget if tries,
Those looks far more than sweetness
  That beameth from their eyes?

I saw those brilliant dark eyes
    Like diamonds in a crest,
But the eyes of fair Juanita
    Out sparkled all the rest.

No wonder that the Padre
    Had sought to gain her love,
To win it, brightest angels
    Would have fallen from above.

I knew I had been musing,
    Of what did scarcely know,
Turned to leave the ruins,
    But could not, could not go.

A form was standing near me,
    All other forms were gone,
I knew it was the "Lost One,"
    The "Lost One" of San Juan.

Then in her own sweet language,
    A little prayer was given,
And sung a song so sweetly,
    That both were heard in heaven.

The song was to her mother
    In words so sweet and clear,
And then she sung another,
    To mother Mary dear.

"Oh mother, take your darling,
 Oh take her home to rest,
Oh take me mother Mary
 With you among the blest.

"I see your spirits standing
 Beside the gates of gold,
While I am lone and weary,
 The night it groweth cold.

"Oh mothers, take your darling,
 I know, I know you will,"
Her sweet sung notes had ended,
 An ever living trill.

And as she ceased her singing,
 Her gentle head had bowed,
While round her like a rainbow
 Arched a golden cloud;

And just amid the archway,
 I saw two mothers stand,
Each looking down with pity,
 Each reaching forth a hand.

While sweet and plaintive singer
 With steadfast gaze above,
Was lifted from her kneeling
 And drawn as 'twere by love.

To arms of Mary mother,
    To arms of mother own ;
The budding earthly blossom,
    In heaven-land had blown.

I know those words are answered,
    " Where has Juanita gone ?"
She's living with the angels,
    That "Lost One" of San Juan.

# WHERE IS SOLITUDE?

Alone, alone, full many a day,
I've traveled o'er cold mountains grey,
Thro' tangled brush, up ledges steep,
'Cross Cañons, yawning, dark and deep,
Till night drew on ; alone I've stood
In forest wild, 'mid solitude :
The solitude of loneliness,
As found in mountain wilderness.

But yet there is no solitude
To me, in lonely mountain wood,
Like that that's found in cities great,
Where thousand people congregate ;
Where all along the crowded street,
A thousand different faces meet,
While not a single face I see,
Gives friendly beck or nod to me.

## FAIR PROSPECTS.

Oft on the street I've hoped, but vain,
To find some look 'twere not for gain ;
But man of wealth with face as cold
As are his sordid heaps of gold ;
And haughty dame was at his side,
Who once had been a laughing bride,
But now no laugh or joy was there,
Each face was furrowed deep with care,
And so it was along the street,
With every face I'd pass or meet.

The men all had some weight of care ;
E'en school-girls too, with faces fair,
If smile would give to passing friend,
That smile would only seem to lend
A deeper shade on saddened brow,
And thus it seemed to me somehow,
That city's crowds have care and sadness,
While forest wilds are full of gladness.

I heard a church bell's welcome tone,
And thought no more I'll feel alone ;
Among God's children there is found,
One friendly place on earthly ground ;
Its lofty spire rose towards the cloud,
Its very walls seemed haughty, proud ;

In I passed and down the aisle,
When usher came with cold church smile,
" The pews are taken, all in here,
Please find a seat back in the rear."
Back I turned with inward moan,
In city's hive I'm still alone.

The preacher prayed long and loud,
The people sat, no heads were bowed,
They'd bought their pews, all cushioned nice,
Bought that prayer at moneyed price ;
While long, cold faces seemed to nod,
" I've bought heaven, can buy my God."
Thoughts were business, not of prayer,
Else sweet humility were there.

A hymn was sung in key so high,
Its fine pitched notes must reach the sky,
To tell the angel with his lyre,
" Behold our operatic choir ;
Your heavenly notes are far more cold
Than our's that's bought with notes of gold;
And when we come we'll bring our choir,
And organ for your tuneless lyre."

The preacher spoke as mind enslaved ;
"I think your chances to be saved
Are growing greater every day,
Because you walk the heavenly way
In the broad path of golden peace,
I have laid down since that increase
Of lucre to your worthy servant ;
To be less truthful, but more fervent."

Then plates were passed to gather coin,
A part of service all could join ;
A sinner's dime is same as others,
If doeth good, equals brothers ;
Why not then preach ? Oh that you would,
"Pure Christian work is doing good ;"
Yes, charity is what we need,
'Tis the true gospel spite of creed.

I staid until the benediction,
Leaving church with this conviction,
"God's true temple is the grove,"
There songs you hear are songs of love ;
In Nature's church no glittering gold
Will pay for prayer that's bought and sold.
No, let me back to lonely wood,
And flee the city's solitude.

Oft I've camped in mountain wild,
But not alone, kind nature smiled;
Each swinging bough, on fr'endly tree,
Gave recognition sweet to me;
Each waving branch however high,
Sang sweet cadenced lullaby,
And thro' the night would vigils keep,
To fan me to a welcome sleep.
No, no, there is no solitude
For me in lonely mountain wood.

Kind nature formed her children all,
From pine-tree great to human small,
In one same mould, the mould of love,
And wrote her gospel in the grove.
"Give friendly welcome each to each,"
But 'tis no use for me to preach,
The love for greed, the love for gold
Hath made mankind more sordid, cold,
Than coldest rock in mountain land,
For its soft moss' a welcome hand,
Which ne'er you'll find, more's the pity
In solitude of a great city.

# UP AND DOWN HILL.

There was an old fellow lived under the hill,
From latest advices is living there still :
Once by an invite I stopped at his place,
Found an honest heart, like his honest face.

He had his own farm and lived at his ease,
With his own bread and butter, made his own cheese,
Ground his own grain, for he owned the old mill
And never had strove to get farther up hill.

At that time two roads ran along by his farm,
But one of the roads had a wonderful charm,
Each traveler rushing along as to kill ;
They were all making money, "going up hill."

It was a broad road and easy to travel,
With nice shady walks, strewn with white gravel,
But none stopped to look at shade, lawn or rill,
'Twas hurry along, we are "going up hill."

All were very polite in helping of others,
One family there, they were all loving brothers ;
If any should fall and valuables spill,
They'd make him up more, "he is going up hill."

All along by the way, none scarcely would stop,
It was such a fine place to live on the top,
They could dwell there forever taking their ease
And never be troubled by poor folks or fleas.

Yes, to live on the top was indeed sublime,
But dissatisfaction was still on the climb ;
As none could get higher, there was no more hill,
Went climbing each other with hearty good will.

As natural upshot, some had to go down ;
While living up there, it was, "dear Mr. Brown,"
But now he had started, each voice loud and shrill,
"Give Old Brown a kick, he's going down hill."

And whoever met him along on the road,
Would readily give him a thrust, punch or goad,
They all did it, too, with such hearty good will,
"Give the old cuss a kick, he's going down hill."

Thus on down the hill with a thump, bump, or thud,
Till down to the bottom to wallow in mud ;
No difference how hungry, sore, sick or ill,
He hadn't a friend anywhere on the hill.

By watching those roads I came to conclusion,
That climbing up hill was worse than delusion,
And I left my old friend at the door of his mill,
Quite thankful indeed, I had not tried the hill.

# THE TIMES.

A spat at the "Times," is what we claim,
   And will speak about high and low station,
   Men who defraud the people and nation—
But whence to strike out to find our first game?
On whom shall be placed the mantle of shame?
Who are the big dogs that are most to blame?
   These are debatable questions.

'Tis the "Press," of course, that opens our eyes,
   The press that is styled "Independent,"
   Sets itself up as the peoples' defendant—
Day in and day out, we hear their long cries,
Each one is barking, from large to small size,
They're going to blast the blood sucking flies;
   But will they keep off the new swarm?

Monopoly has his grasp at our throat,
   Squeezing our necks in its corporate vice,
   Saying, "I'll make you come to my price—
If you wish to ride on my cars or my boat
I must have the money, can't take your note,
If I am bloated, I wont take nary bloat,
   Unless he shall pay for a ticket."

Suppose Mr. Growler should buy boat and road,
  Would he give us cheap freight and riding,
  Because with the people he had been siding?
We are rather thinking his lash and goad
Would find a sting in new business mode,
And we'd be fearful of him, as the toad
  Who now is the boss of the puddle.

The Government's rotten, down to the core,
  The thieving we know is on the immense ;
  Why don't every growler talk common sense?
And stop their senseless unmeaning roar,
Let them talk cause, for cause comes before
The body politic can have any sore :
  Reform must begin at the bottom.

If we were all honest our troubles would end,
  But so long as we worship Old Mammon,
  It's all bosh ; yes, infernal gammon,
To think the world's wickedness ever will end,
But to hook or crook each place-man will bend,
No difference if saints to Congress we send,
  They'll sell out at some price or other.

# ISLE OF SANTA ROSA.

On Isle of Santa Rosa
A little valley cosy,
Where breeze from Southern Ocean
    Bringeth tropic odors sweet ;
Where each little wavelet's motion
    In music cadenced beat,
    Are ever, ever telling
    With love our hearts are welling
    While expiring at your feet.

    The tidal wave is nearing,
    In pretty valleys' hearing,
" Our crystal arms shall grasp you,"
    Speaketh now the little waves,
" Yes, our sea-girt arms shall clasp you,
    Till your green-sward bosom laves
    With limpid, sparkling water,
    Thou pretty Islands' daughter,
    No more we'll be your slaves."

To valley, from bold highland,
　　Speaks back old father Island ;
" I shall guard thee, lovely daughter,
　　Cease thy fearing evermore ;
There are bounds to ocean's water,
　　I have bound it with my shore."
To Island, waves are heeding,
Then backward, back receding,
Till as distant as before.

Along the pebbly white sand,
　　'Round pretty valley's bright land,
I've watched the heaving ocean,
　　In its grandeur, might and pride ;
Earth's pendulum giving motion,
　　With the sun and moon to guide ;
So far toward land-ward beating,
Thence seaward till completing
One pulse of Time and Tide.

# LONG YEARS AGO.

Long years ago I knew a child,
Who had been formed in beauty's mould,
With soft blue eyes, so fair and mild,
That when she passed the roses smiled,
    And would her little form enfold
    In scented robes that all the gold
In placer land would fail to buy—
The roses knew the reason why.

They loved the one of whom I speak,
    The little birdlings did the same,
For she was gentle, kind and meek,
A smile for all shone on her cheek;
    And e'en the wild deer often came,
    While playful fawn with her was tame,
And ran to meet her without fear,
Two happy loves, the "deer" and "dear."

'Tis said such fair ones need die young,
  But that sweet child more lovely grew,
Till every heart and every tongue,
But spoke her praise, her beauty sung,
  In adoration's worship true—
  Thus years passed, and ere I knew,
That child to me was child no more,
But woman lovlier than before.

The picture's formed, the budding rose
  To highest life had fully blown,
Its hidden beauties to disclose
In type the Great Creator chose
  For woman, and for her alone—
  So fair indeed, that angels own,
And often do, I b'lieve, repine
For form like hers, a form divine.

I'd watched the bud, beheld the flower,
  Loved them both and love them still,
With undying, lasting power
That's not dimmed by passing shower,
  Which often doth cold passion kill,—
  Pure love's formed from mind and will,
Is not a passion, far more high,
'Tis part of soul, 'twill never die.

The flower I speak was never mine,
   Neither is yon glittering star,
Yet I behold its beauties shine,
Can love its light and ne'er repine,
   Because I am from it so far ;
   That never doth its beauties mar—
The bud, the flower, and star above,
I love them all, they're mine to love.

## A POET'S THEME.

A poet who was courting Fame,
   Travers'd the world to find a Theme,
'Twould build himself Byronic name,
That should all modern muses shame.
   He searched the banks of fiction's stream,
   Would craze by day, at night would dream,
From Egypt's Nile to Tiber's Rome ;
Poor fellow, left his theme at home.

What he has left we'll sing it o'er;
A pretty maid once fair and free,
Her home was near a northern shore,
The songs she heard, the breaker's roar,
　The cold, cold waves from northern sea,
　E'er sung her chorus, "woe is me,
He cometh not, I've waited long,"
But lo, she hears his distant song,

And turns her gaze towards eastern hill,
　To see the ideal of her soul
Descending thro' the coast fog chill :
Her pure warm heart, its beatings still,
　'Tis nearing towards a maidens' goal
　Like little boat on breaker's shoal—
Will he who comes do manly part
To save the boat and bless the heart?

No doubt he is some hero bold,
　But time will every story tell,
His heart then young, had e'en grown old
In love affairs, till it was cold
　As lava beds, where then did dwell,
　Blood of his veins, bright half-breed Belle.
Such was the man, such his renown,
　Who'd come to win a Myrtle crown.

## FAIR PROSPECTS.

A hero of the backwoods, look,
  No ermined suit deigned to wear,
His dressing mirror was the brook,
Yet he was proud, what pains had took
  With his long, floating yellow hair,
  While pistol belt was slung with care ;
Huge spurs to wake his pinto barb,
Such was our hero, such his garb.

He came, they met, sweet river-side,
  Oh, what a bright poetic theme ;
She, loved, was soon a happy bride,
And he was happy in his pride—
  Such blissful conquest scarce did dream ;
  Then why not poetize the stream ?
In vain may seek in distant Rome,
For theme like that he left at home.

# GARDEN OF TRUTH.

This world is a world of fault finding,
    And whoever truth would expound,
Will find out the subject is binding,—
    He's tramping on dangerous ground.

Is tramping on ground of the teacher,
    On somebody's toes and sore corns,
On harrow'd up ground of the preacher,
    And with ev'ry saint, must lock horns.

The merchant and old speculator,
    Have each laid a claim on the soil,
While church, with its huge perforator,
    Is boring the balance for "oil."

So is it, with each occupation,
    Should I name and class them by lot,
The ground is all claimed in creation
    Excepting one lone little spot.

That lone spot with no one to claim it,
   Tho' taught to remember in youth,
As you will admit when I name it,
   The old fashioned Garden of Truth.

The teacher hath torn down the palings;
   The saint hath sold out at a price;
The preacher rail'd loud in his railings
   Against the encroachment of vice;

But call he received from "Old Lucre,"
   His share in the garden was sold;
The Devil knows how to play "euchre,"
   And best place to scatter his gold.

Both merchant and old speculator
   Have long since forsaken the place,
While church, just a little while later,
   Mortgaged its last hold to grace.

The garden now nearly forsaken,
   Like grave-yard we pass in the night—
But from each shall new life awaken
   To shine, with an eternal light.

# SONGS OF THE PAST.

How many old stories unwritten,
 How many sweet songs of the past
Are floating around us like sunbeams—
 Like sunbeams forever to last.

For each brilliant thought of the thinker,
 And every sweet song that's been sung,
Like the seeds that earth surely garners,
 Are germs from which blossoms have sprung.

For Nature can ne'er lose an atom,
 Tho' changing its form at her will,
It remains a part of creation,
 Its own proper functions to fill.

Oh, thinker, think not all for present,
 Your thoughts either low or sublime,
Are building up minds for the future,
 To blossom through unending time.

Sweet singer, your songs shall grow sweeter,
 Each year, as the year taketh pace,
And the notes you are singing to-day shall
 Be music for those in your place.

Our words, our thoughts and our actions,
   Conceal them how well we may try,
Are parts of eternal creation
   That never can wither or die.

How pure then should be thought and action,
   Improving whilever we can,
The mind which remaineth undying,
   'Tis the soul, and true soul of man.


## CHEROKEE FLAT.

If you never seen deep diggings, like those at Cherokee,
'Twill surely pay to go there—what a sight you'll see,
It's worth a year's travel, 'twill only take a day,
And neither time nor money will be thrown away.

From Oroville, conveyance, or foot it 'round the hill,
The mountain air's bracing, you'll travel with a will—
Yes, the air is bracing—but surely you'll agree,
It's an up-hill business—a walk to Cherokee.

When on Table Mountain you'll hear an ocean roar,
As tho' angry breakers were beating 'gainst a shore—
But 'tis not ocean's breakers, as you'll shortly see,
But the mountain breakers, round the flat at Cherokee.

You've heard of the Dutchman, who had a pipe so large
That 'twas often chartered for a boat or barge—
Once he ventured in it and crossed the Zuyder Zee,
That pipe's no comparison to the pipes at Cherokee.

They laid across bold cañons—cañons deep and wide,
Down from mountain's summit and up the other side—
There's no use o' talking, the work is on immense,
And it took engineering o' brains chock full o' sense.

The work was done by miners, quite a common thing,
When they wish for water—water they will bring—
Here 'twas flowing rivers, 'twould feed an inland sea,
To wash away the mountains around old Cherokee.

Go into the diggin's—what think you? Well, no odds,
To me there's appearance of the destroying gods—
Who are leveling hills down they had reared of yore,
To tell us mountains were, but shall be no more.

Forced water from engines, hissing white as steam,
By hydraulic pressure to hurl a mighty stream—
Speaking the language of imprisoned thunder,
Lookout for safer footing—better get from under.

Down comes tumbling mountains of auriferous gravel,
Bowlders and pebbles have started on their travel,
Each hurries with the other, jumping into flume,
And hardly say "good morning," till in darkened gloom.

Soon from mouth of tunnel plunging with a crash,
Well, they are rock-bound, or every bone would mash—
In plunge there's no resting, their place is down below,
The flume is before them and the cry is, "still we go."

Same as tramping miners, blankets on their shoulders,
Ever traveling onward like the rolling bowlders—
May stop in whirling eddy, but soon will hurry past,
Till at death's dump-pile—some tramp must be our last.

I could tell more, of flumes reaching for miles,
Of the gold they wash out—simply "piles" and "piles"—
But I cannot do it justice—just go yourself and see,
And you'll never wish you hadn't went up to Cherokee.

# WASHED THROUGH A TUNNEL.

"I war washed through a forty foot tunnel,
   Got knocked by a pipe in the flume,
   Kin prove it by a man in the room ;
That feller thar, whose throat is a funnel ;
   After drinkin', he'll "hark from the tomb ;"
Joe, warn't I washed through a forty foot tunnel ?

" Better stop your old gas-pipe from blowin',
   The thing war just played for a joke :"
   "Played ? It war lucky my head warn't broke."
" Well I know how you must o' felt goin,'
   Didn't I have my old carcuss in soak ;
In a place wus nor a forty foot tunnel ?

"Sir, you've seed the big Cherokee pipe ;
   A mile long, if it is ary inch,
   The thought on it still makes me scrinch,
An' gives my old body a touch o' the gripe,
   Like a hoss when you draw on the cinch :
That pipe's eight hundred foot o' depression.

"An' sir, I div through it once on a bet,
  The bet war a gallon o' whisky ;
  But the thing war almoughty risky ;
Yes sir, I feel its effects most till yet ;
  Shall never again be so frisky
As I war 'fore that awful compression.

" At a speed on a whole mile a minute,
  That pipe carries five thousand inches ;"
'Dove through it ?  The shoe rather pinches :'
" Pinch ?  You'd ha' thought so had you been in it,
  Cinched up by them five thousand cinches ;
I did it, kin prove it, Jim held the stakes.

" When I div, didn't water roar in my head ?
  How it gurgled my old throat ter fill,
  Glad I warn't like a fish with a gill,
Or I'd swallered enough to went dead,
  An' could never had writ my last will ;
But I held my breath, for Jim held the stakes.

"Good Lord, but didn't I go through thar spinnin',
  Like a shot from a big Parrot gun,
  Wished it over 'fore it bergun ;
Sir, 'taint no use at all on your grinnin',
  I could prove it the time it war done,
Why Jim kin tell you, for he held the stakes.

"If I went down like a voice from the tomb,
  I ris up like I'd ris frum the dead,
'Twar a close shave o' meetin' Old Ned,
When the boys fished me out on the flume—
  'Jim, he ain't dead,' the fust words they said,
'Give him some stakes if he ain't won the bet.'

" Will I drink ? Of course, I'm dry as a fish,
  Never refuse when it ar goin',
But hope you don't think I war blowin',
I allus did have a hankerin' wish
  Ter tell somebody'd give it a showin',
I could tell it all night ; but sir, here's luck."

## LINE OF THE DITCH.

The line of the ditch we were bringing along,
  Bursting the bowlders and blasting the ledge,
The click of the hammers from arms stout and strong,
  Answering echoes to thuds of the sledge ;

## FAIR PROSPECTS.

When the Foreman came by,
With outstriding walk,
'Twas a glance of his eye,
Said, "Boys, make her talk,
The ditch must be finished this Fall."

Along the whole line an unceasing roar,
Like a fortress repelling a foe,
While high o'er the tree-tops the broken rocks soar,
The powder has given them tickets to go;
And the Foreman who's nigh,
Is filled with delight,
With that look from his eye,
Of, "boys, I am right,
The ditch will be finished this Fall."

Thus to the end the last hole was drilled,
The Foreman was there and would load it
With "giant" and "black," had it part filled,
"Crash!"—Jack spoke, "poor fellow, I know'd it."
While the Foreman was nigh,
But oh, what a sight,
With Death's glare on his eye,
Which said, "Boys, all's right,
I've finished the ditch and done it this Fall."

# THE GRANGER'S DAUGHTER.

I'm old enough and should have sense,
    'Twould keep me out of trouble,
Were not my feelings on immense
    To hanker for a double.
And that's the reason as is seen,
    I ran my neck in danger,
'Twas all thro' love for Dolly Green,
    The daughter of a Granger.

CHORUS:

Sweet Dolly Green, of San Joaquin,
    She did my life endanger,
I lost my suit, but won a boot
    From the foot of an old Granger.

Her father owned a pretty farm,
    'Twas close beside Joaquin,
No other ranch had half the charm,
    'Twas charmed by Dolly Green.
I can't tell how I first got there,
    I was almost a stranger,
But sight of Dolly made me swear
    I'd live and die a Granger.

CHORUS: Sweet Dolly Green, &c.

So hiring out to father Green,
    I'd help him cut his grain,
The finest crop that e'er was seen
    Upon the Joaquin plain.
I rose to labor with the sun,
    Tho' tired I'd still be jolly,
For well I knew when work was done
    I'd get a smile from Dolly.

CHORUS:

    Sweet Dolly Green, &c.

I helped to cut and thrash the crop,
    And days were bright and happy,
Until I did the question pop,
    She smiling said, "ask pa-pa."
To her dear pa, an abject slave
    I pleading pressed my suit,
The only answer that he gave,
    Was with his stogy boot.

CHORUS:

    Sweet Dolly Green, of San Joaquin,
        She did my life endanger,
    I lost my suit, but won a boot
        From the foot of an old Granger.

Among you folks who think I'm green,
    And was laid on the shelf,
You'd better go to San Joaquin
    And try it on yourself.
If you should seek sweet Dolly's hand,
    You'll get your nose in danger,
Besides will aptly understand
    The standing of a Granger.

CHORUS:

Sweet Dolly Green of San Joaquin,
    She did my life endanger,
I lost my suit, but won a boot
    From the foot of an old Granger.

## LIVING ALONE

I had lived alone in the wild mountains drear,
    Five years and a-half, to a day,
But something kept whispering, ever would say,
    "Why be so foolish as longer to stay
In this lonesome place year after year?"

" Why thus be spending the whole of your life,
  While hardly are living at best,
  And ceasing your labor scarcely have rest;
  The reason is plain, easily guessed,
A woman could answer the question—a wife.

" Had you hunted for one as you've hunted for gold,
  And put half your work on a farm,
  You'd now have a home and something to charm,
  And something besides to hold in your arm,
Some bright little flowerets of year or more old."

No wonder such thoughts would whisper to mind;
  During that time no bright form was seen,
  No fluttering dress of white, pink or green,
  As carried around by six or sixteen,
Or anything else as shaped woman-kind.

True, I'd companions, but one thing must own,
  Men living thus nearly cease to be human,
  A fact that will be disputed by few men,
  And living where you never see woman,
I said it, and mean it, 'twas "living alone."

# BRUNETTE JOSIE.

Long years ago, how long you'll know,
    When I tell, Santa Rosa
Was then so small, ten houses all—
    But one held Brunette Josie.
        Talk of your girls with golden curls,
            And cheeks so fair and rosy,
        But none there are that can compare
            To my lost Brunette Josie.

I'd traveled round each mountain town
    From Butte to Mariposa,
But in that round had never found
    So fair a lass as Josie.
        Talk of your girls with raven curls,
            And cheeks so fair and rosy,
        But none there are that can compare
            To my lost Brunette Josie.

Long years have fled, and my old head
    Is getting old and dozy,
Full many a queen mine eye hath seen,
    But none so fair as Josie.
        Talk of your girls with flowing curls,
            And cheeks so bright and rosy,
        But none there are that can compare
            To my lost Brunett Josie.

# THE ROAD OF LIFE.

That road we all travel, the road of our life,
   Which each one doth build as he goes,
Some dig it thro' toilings, some bridge it with strife,
   And some make it how nobody knows.

There is but once passing along this same road,
   Tho' there may be sameness each day,
Every step's nearing that resting abode,
   The last little hillock of clay.

From Here to Hereafter is but a short span,
   There's no coming back to help others,
Then journeying along, let us do what we can
   To level the road for our brothers.

Our path may be rugged for mile upon mile,
   And hunger and want be severe,
How often it is an encouraging smile
   Will roll back a gathering tear.

Then let us be helpful, and help while we may,
   For the night it cometh on fast,
We only can work while yet is day,
   Our actions are gone in the past.

# MY PICTURE.

I sought the wild mountains, my occupation
    Was hunting bright landscapes, not game,
Determined my brush should form a creation,
That would give me name, honor and station,
    Along-side of others in niches of fame.

I tasted and drank as nature's true lover,
    From her sweet offerings everywhere found,
Though pages of grandeur I kept turning over,
New leaves would open and beauty still hover,
    To guard lovely pictures, that she had crowned.

A bright little streamlet thro' green-sward prairie,
    Murmured from woodlands shaded above,
Whence sweet singing birds, not caged up canary,
But joyous in freedom, in concert so merry,
    Were trilling glad music of nature and love.

To sketch it, I knew would be cold imitation,
    Dropping my pencil, I hurried away,
With thoughts I had found, but left my creation,
Left it because I felt inspiration—
    "God's finished pictures no art can portray."

# UNCLE JOE AND THE GRIZZLY.

Did you never hear tell 'bout that ar' fight
   Twixt Uncle Joe, I an' the grizzly?
It happened a little arter daylight,
   'The mornin' had sot in dern'd drizzly.

Uncle Joe an' I war keepin' a ranch,
   At an openin' up thar in the woods,
Our hog-pen stood jist across a small branch,
   An' a stock o' them brutes, all on our goods.

We war up quite airly, finished our meal,
   Sat dozing away in the corner,
When thar war a noise, a hog 'gan ter squeal,
   Says Uncle Joe, "He ar' a goner."

He kotch'd up the rifle, slung on the pouch,
   And soon war long tracks a makin',
You can bet yer life Uncle Joe warn't a slouch,
   He meant it; ter save our live bacon.

I hadn't no gun, so I took up the axe,
   But my knees war so weak, I went slow;
No use ter conceal—I'm statin' the facts—
   'Bout a bar fight, 'taint no use ter blow.

I war near enough ter see how it war;
    He snapped, the derned gun wouldn't go;
They both come tergether, him an' the bar,—
    'Twar a sight ter see Uncle Joe.

He jist gin a scream, an Arkansaw leap,
    He'd judged on the chances with car;
They both rolled over thar in a heap,
    But Joe war on top of the bar.

The brute he war skeer'd an' started ter run;
    Oh warn't he a git up an' gitter;
I don't know which on 'em had the most fun,
    Uncle Joe war riding the critter.

Left thar all alone, I felt pokish bad,
    My eyes like the mornin' war drizzly,
But one thing ar' certain, I war almoughty glad
    'Twarn't me 'twar riding old grizzly.

---

From that day ter this, I solemn declar',
    I've heard nothin' from poor Uncle Joe;
Did he swoller him, or him eat the bar?
    That ar' what I'd still like ter know!

# GOOD DICK.

Good Dick, at home, the parson's heir,
    Had been brought up in morals true,
Was trained in church with pious care,
To never cheat, or lie, or swear ;
    But Dick, poor boy, perhaps like you,
    Once had to bid his pa adieu.
The parson gave his boy the blessing,
They parted—well, 'twas quite distressing.

Moons came and went, and lo, Good Dick
    Had pitched his tent in mining land,
He thought of work, but then the pick
Was not the thing—it made him sick ;
    In fact his smooth white surfaced hand
    Was made for something far more grand.
Dick's head, like ours, was quite prodigious,
Containing bumps 'twere irreligious.

Instead of laboring for his gold,
    He chose the pretty game of chance,
And wrote unto his papa old,
And here's the words sweet sonny told :
    "Dear father, I've made great advance ;
Instead of wielding Christian lance,
I've learned an art, took little teaching ;
'Twould pay you better, pa, than preaching."

The parson pondered as he read,
    And then began his duds to pack ;
Somehow he had an inward dread,
That Dick might not the right path tread,
    And he must go and put him back
    Into the moral Christian track.
He gave his brethren all a blest word ;
Next morning found him going west-ward.

On train, towards the setting sun,
    O'er plains and mountains fast he sped ;
But ere his journey was half done,
Good mission work he had begun.
    A Monte-sharp, his cards had spread,
    When gentle parson kindly said :
"My dear young man, in Christian feeling,
I pray desist thine wicked dealing."

The young man seemed touched at heart,
"Good sir, a penitent you see;
Yet by this most nefarious art,
I've won the wealth 'twould college start,
  And you shall have it just as free,
  As are these cards upon my knee.
'Twill build a church or rear a college,
To teach men moral, useful knowledge.

"I'll give it free, I'll give it all,
  You see the 'mount that's in the stack,
If you will simply turn and call
This little card—you see how small's
  The work to do;—yes that is jack,
  A child could turn it every whack;
The gold is yours in shortest metre,
I'll stake it all 'gainst thine repeater."

At first the parson looked with pain,
  But seeing such an easy thing,
So fair a chance for wordly gain,
Down went the golden watch and chain.
  He saw the jack, the ace and king,
  Turned a card—his watch took wing;
The gambler said, "My dear old croaker,
You failed to find the 'little joker.'"

The parson's face turned blue and red,
   His knees were weak, his heart grew sick,
Besides, felt dizzy in his head,
Like fainting patient badly bled.
   The sharp then spoke : "Dear pa, this trick
   Is played by thy beloved Dick,
You see my pile of useful knowledge,
Let's take it home and build a college."

### THE MORAL

Amounts to this, which had you rather
Be a bad boy or good old father?

## SLIPPERY JIM.

"Never hearn tell 'bout Slippery Jim?
   Good chap, he war, no mistaken,
Died mighty queer, couldn't reach an oak limb,
Tried it so hard—his feet sorter clim'—
That war the last which I seed o' him—
   Hangin' up thar like smoked bacon.

" Poor Jim war a chap which didn't mean harm,
  Had ways that war rather takin',
Whatever'd come in reach of his arm
Would stick ter his claws jist like a charm—
Chick on a roost, or hog on a farm—
  He war lightnin' you bet, on live bacon.

" Allus did well while stayin' round here,
  Nice fortin' he war o' makin';
The thing in my mind h'aint exactly clear—
The fact on it ar' Jim acted blamed queer,—
Reckon he hadn't the least bit o' fear
  He ever would lose his own bacon.

"Made his last deal; the dern'd China breed,
  Nothin' ter make a good rakin',
Go on the skeer, never orter use bleed,
Make 'em shell out every time, the 'kale-seed ;"
No use o' talkin', Jim hadn't the need
  Ter salt down any such bacon.

" How'd it come ? Don't know; thar I seed
  Desperit efforts o' makin';
His arms couldn't quite reach up ter the limb,
Tried it so hard—his feet sorter clim'—
That war the last o' poor Slippery Jim—
  Hangin' up thar like smoked bacon."

# HAPPY JACK.

I 'spose you've hearn o' Happy Jack,
   Well known in Fifty-two;
The gold he dug would fill a sack,
So large 'twould take a mule to pack
   One half the dust—that's true.

He'd been a sailor chap, 'twar said,
   An old salt water duck,
But somehow got it in his head,
He'd leave his ship and pilot bread,
   A land cruise take for luck.

When reached the mines, he war flat broke,
   Without a single red;
But nary time he didn't croak,
Jist put his boots an' coat in soak
   For whisky—not for bread.

Then looked about, found an old pick,
   An' started out for luck,
Went waddling down along the creek,
And never made the second lick,
   The fust dab—why he struck

A chunk that weighed nigh fifty pound,
  Nor never looked for more,
War satisfied with what he'd found ;
So calling all us fellers round,
  He jist bought out the store.

But wouldn't sell the fust dern'd thing ;
  Said, boys, "Here's plenty o' truck ;
We've got enough ter last till spring,
An' when it's gone, why then, by jing !
  We'll go it high fur luck."

We all pitched in, oh what a spree,
  I think on it till yet ;
Whisky flowed, the grub war free,
Oh warn't Old Jack in highest glee,
  The happiest dog you bet.

That's fust I know'd o' Happy Jack,
  True heart—he war no sham,
But business getting sorter slack,
Poor fellow shouldered up his pack
  And went to—Yuba d—m.

# CURLEY DAN.

Our partner's name was Curley Dan,
   His twisted locks had gave his name ;
He somehow didn't like the plan
Of working like an honest man,
   So selling out his part of the claim,
   He started out to hunt the game.
"Good bye," he said, "my honest pards,
I'm off to try my luck at cards."

We heard of him in many a fray,
   Amid the central mining range,
He battled most with "duce and tray,"
Sometimes would deal, sometimes would play
   A hand most wond'rous, passing strange,
   But it would win the miner's change.
Until 'twas noised from man to man,
"The devil plays for Curley Dan."

One night the game was running steep,
   That means they were not betting small ;
For nights and days ther'd been no sleep,
'Twas "ante," "rake," "come here, barkeep,
   Whisky 'round for one and all,"
   'Most every time a hand they'd call.
But all in vain, each bet they'd make,
   'Twas Curley Dan who'd win the stake.

He broke them all, then with a boast,
   " Who's here to play with Curley Dan ?
I'll play the Devil or his ghost
And beat him, too—if I don't roast
   My liver." A strange form, old and wan,
   With husky voice, spoke, " I'm your man."
Down they sat in players places,
The cards were dealt, Dan held four aces.

A bet, a raise, " I'll go you higher "—
   Dan's all was up, he called " a sight,"
The stranger's eyes were lit with fire,
" No sight for you, thou wicked liar,
   That's not your all, I claim the right
   To make you play your life to-night."
Dan swore an oath, 'twas his last breath,
Laid down four aces—beat by Death.

www.ingramcontent.com/pod-product-compliance
Lightning Source LLC
Chambersburg PA
CBHW020253170426

43202CB00008B/352